M000206857

Lost Restaurants

OF

FAIRFIELD, CALIFORNIA

Lost Restaurants

OF

FAIRFIELD, CALIFORNIA

TONY WADE

AMERICAN PALATE

Published by American Palate
A Division of The History Press
Charleston, SC
www.historypress.com

Copyright © 2022 by Tony Wade
All rights reserved

Front cover, clockwise from top left: Voici. *Courtesy of Irving Scible.* Sid's Drive-In. *Courtesy of Donna Covey Paintings.* Sara's Pancakes. *Courtesy of Karen Bennett Moore.* Dan & Ruth's Cafe. *Armijo High yearbook, 1969.*
Back cover, top: Rockville Corner Inn. *Armijo High yearbook, 1965.*
Back cover, bottom: Eastern Café. *Armijo High yearbook, 1963.*

First published 2022

Manufactured in the United States

ISBN 9781467152259

Library of Congress Control Number: 2022935415

Notice: The information in this book is true and complete to the best of our knowledge. It is offered without guarantee on the part of the author or The History Press. The author and The History Press disclaim all liability in connection with the use of this book.

All rights reserved. No part of this book may be reproduced or transmitted in any form whatsoever without prior written permission from the publisher except in the case of brief quotations embodied in critical articles and reviews.

To the bygone Solano County seat restauranteurs who, over the decades, nourished the bodies, hearts and souls of generations of Fairfielders.

Contents

Meals and Memory

We all have our food memories, some good and some bad. The taste, smell and texture of food can be extraordinarily evocative, bringing back memories not just of eating the food itself but also of the place and setting in which the food was consumed. Beyond memories of taste and place, food is effective as a trigger of even deeper memories of feelings and emotions, internal states of the mind and body. These kinds of memories can sneak up on you: they have the power to derail a current train of thought and replace it with one both unexpected and unexpectedly potent.
—*John S. Allen,* The Omnivorous Mind:
Our Evolving Relationship with Food

In my first book, *Growing Up in Fairfield, California,* there is a chapter titled "Let's Eat!" It was inspired by the fact that in the ten-thousand-plus-member-strong Facebook group "I Grew Up in Fairfield, Too" that I coadministrate, so many of the threads people discuss end up defaulting to food.

Now, to be sure, many posts in the group are primarily about old eateries from the past that now only exist in the internal memory reels of locals. Others are seemingly unrelated but end up there all the same. I mean, someone could be talking about "slammin' a homer outta Lee Bell Park" when they played Little League, and the memory would include the Sham's Pizza party afterward.

Downtown Fairfield with the Palace Grill on the left and the Airline Café on the right. *Tim Farmer collection.*

If a member brought up how much they missed shopping at Fairfield's 1960s proto-Walmart superstore Wonder World, someone was sure to bring up the donuts that were baked fresh in the bakery.

Heck, some locals even wax nostalgic about the submarine sandwiches at the old Kmart cafeteria for crying out loud!

So when I was contemplating a follow-up book, my acquisitions editor from The History Press, Laurie Krill, bounced an idea off me. Books she said were popular in other areas were Lost Restaurants titles. She sent me a few sample PDFs, and while I was intrigued, I had a few reasons to pump the brakes a little.

I mean, the samples I perused more often than not dealt with restaurants that were more of the snooty, high-falutin' variety. Don't get me wrong, Fairfield has had (and still has) some of those, but by and large, it was and is a burgers and good ol 'American food town. I, like most Fairfielders, am totally cool with that.

I also definitely perceived some real challenges involved in pursuing such a project. One of the features I insist on is including the many remembrances culled from Facebook by locals that are memorable, humorous and thought-provoking. However, many times, posts about bygone restaurants simply say something along the lines of "I loved that place!" or "Man, I miss their tacos!" or "Best soft serve ice cream ever!"

Try reading 208 pages of that.

So I was leaning toward a different book, but a couple of things kept pulling me back to the Lost Restaurants. The main draw was the food-memory connection. There is something compelling about the multisensory process of eating that seems interesting to explore, especially using the hyperlocal focus that The History Press/Arcadia Publishing books are known for. That dynamic intersection of meals and memories kept calling to me, and finally in November 2021, I made up my mind and sent in a proposal for this book. It was accepted on—wait for it—the day before Thanksgiving.

One thing that directly led me to the decision was a personal remembrance of a special time spent with my father.

Like many Fairfielders, I am not a native Californian but was brought here because I was a U.S. Navy brat. I spent the first eleven years of my life in Norfolk, Virginia. My parents were very religious, and we went to church several times a week. My father was a deacon, and after the Sunday evening service, he would show Super 8 films for new Christian converts.

In 1975, I used to schlep my dad's old Bell & Howell projector to a classroom, set it up and then afterward take it all down. Now, I didn't do that because I was necessarily a dutiful son or a gung-ho budding Christian. My motivation for helping my dad was not spiritual but gastronomical.

Many Fairfielders fondly recall the cherry Cokes, hot dogs with square buns and banana splits at the downtown Woolworth's Luncheonette. *Armijo yearbook, 1963.*

11

You see, on the way home each Sunday night, my dad and I would stop at Burger King.

The memories of our stops there always seem to play in soft focus when I pull them out of my mind vault to review and savor. I would always order the same thing: a Whaler fish sandwich, large fries and a strawberry shake. When I reflect on it now, the super-hot, fresh-out-of-the-grease deep-fried fish sandwich slathered with tartar sauce was perfectly matched with the salty fries and sweet, creamy shake—pure bliss. I am now aware that my reaction and satisfaction with that meal back then was in large part due to the determined work of food scientists making sure that Burger King's fare was delicious and addictive.

However, part of my rich fondness for replaying that particular memory is that it was also precious one-on-one time with my dad. While we ate, he would ask me how I was doing at school, what my spelling words were for that week, what activities my Cub Scout den was planning and sundry other things that sometimes get short shrift in the busyness of everyday life. My four brothers knew I stayed after church and helped dad with the projector, but our Burger King trips were just between us. Having that personal time with my father was golden.

In author Michael Moss's 2021 book, *Hooked: Food, Free Will, and How the Food Giants Exploit Our Addictions*, he explores this connection:

> *Food resonates so large in our memory because food looms large in our lives. The act of eating touches everything we experience, everywhere we go, everyone we know and everything we feel. As much as we are what we eat, we are what we remember, which explains why most everyone has a food memory that helps define who they are.*

That section reminded me of the 2000 movie *Hi Fidelity* about a record store owner played by John Cusak who is unlucky in love. A friend of his comes over to his apartment and notices that he has his record collection in piles on the floor. He asks Cusak how he is rearranging them—in chronological or alphabetical order—and he replies, "Autobiographical." Like the six degrees of Kevin Bacon phenomenon, he tells his friend he could trace why he did a certain thing in his life using certain records.

It might be a bit of a stretch, but I imagine that if they had access to the menus of several long-ago restaurants that many longtime Fairfielders could arrange them in such a way as to convey a few autobiographical stories as well.

That leads me to another reason why I wanted to write this book, besides the memories of old places where you could get your grub on. There are some interesting stories of restaurant owners and the restaurants themselves that simply have not been told.

I think it's important to state that I'm not trying to impress anybody with our cuisine here. I'm just attempting to convey the importance that certain restaurants and their food had and still have in this community and share the warm and meaningful memories that they trigger in many people. Memories, I might add, that often far outlast the actual restaurants that helped birth them.

I am so thankful for the ten-thousand-plus members of the "I Grew Up in Fairfield, Too" Facebook group. They have shared their memories of local places since the group was founded in 2009 by Rick "The Creator" Williams. The members were, and are, a rich resource of information and connection. I am pleased to have many of their voices represented in this book to help flesh out tales from our collective culinary past.

One thing I must mention is that I was surprised that some people saw the title of my first book and assumed that it was my autobiography. Uh, no. Even I wouldn't want to read that, so why would somebody else? The primary focus of that book and this one, is Fairfield, not me. That said, I do try to add my own flavor from time to time, often with humorous injections into the otherwise "just the facts ma'am" text and most notably in the interludes sprinkled throughout, which are either fictionalized or made out of whole (table)cloth.

This book is about restaurants that no longer exist, and while a lot of bars, taverns and saloons also served food in town, they technically weren't restaurants. Actually, there used to be a California law saying drinking spots had to serve food. In fact, in 1947, fifteen Solano County taverns got dinged by the State Board of Equalization for not serving food at their establishments. Still, for the most part, they are not included in this book.

One of the things that my research showed me was just how entrenched eateries were and are woven into the very fabric of Fairfield. As businesses, they partnered with the community in numerous ways, including advertising in the local newspaper, school newspapers and yearbooks, sponsoring Little League baseball teams, softball squads and bowling teams and helping with special community events. Many folks may not recall that back in the day, the "Church Services" section of the paper was sponsored by Fairfield eateries like Muffin Treat, Pietro's, Johanne's Hot Dogs and other types of businesses.

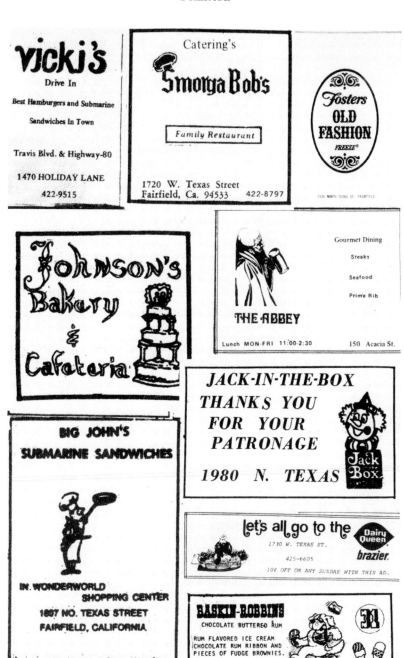

Mid-1970s advertisements in the *Armijo High School Joint Union* school newspaper. *Tim Farmer collection.*

Restaurant owners provided employment for many Fairfielders, which led to customers having personal connections with the people who worked there. I remember how wonderful it was to go to Sandy's 101 Omelettes and not only know that waitress Nikki Couch (may she rest in peace) would know exactly what I wanted, but would be there with a smile and we could chat about everything from sports to politics.

So ultimately, it's not just about the food. I mean, right now, *Star Trek* food replicators are still science fiction, but if we one day have something similar that can re-create many of the dishes from the past that are mentioned within these pages, it still could not replicate the toasty good feelings of spending quality time with family or friends.

Now, I have never actually worked as a server for a restaurant, but the fact that many of you have returned to my writings like a valued loyal customer to an old-school eatery is heartwarming. It is validation that I did my job at least adequately enough with the first effort and that many of you believe— or at least hope—that I can pull it off again.

With my first book, I welcomed you, got your drink order (a Fuzzy Nostalgia on the rocks), gave you the menu, took your order, delivered your food and, finally, after you were sated, presented you with a check.

I consider you reading and enjoying this book as my 20 percent tip.

Thank you so much,
Tony Wade
February 2022

Acknowledgements

In the acknowledgements section of my first book, *Growing Up in Fairfield, California*, I was so juiced at finally being a published author that I thanked everyone I could think of including, literally, my dog.

So rather than repeating myself here, if you are one of the people who are listed in my first effort, please consider yourself rethanked for this book as well.

I must, however, sincerely thank my literal in-house editor, my wife, Beth, for her valiant efforts in helping me to sandblast, tighten and polish my prose.

I also want to give extra props to my brother Kelvin Wade, who has written an opinion column for the *Fairfield Daily Republic* newspaper since 1992 called "The Other Side." I happily rode his coattails, and they definitely helped lead me to this point.

I especially want to thank everyone who bought my first book, those who checked it out from the library (including the anonymous person who evidently ~~stole~~ permanently borrowed a copy) and all those who came by and spoke with me at book signing/selling events. I thought finally getting a book published would be the best part of that experience, but I was wrong. It was hands down how happy the book made so many people. I'd like to give a special shout-out to so many of y'all who bought multiple copies for friends and family. And I'd like to give a super special shout-out to my former Carl's Jr. coworker Lori Rinehart, who bought fifteen copies!

Fist bumps to the Solano County Library. Not only did its staff not flinch as I hoarded their microfilm machines for hours on end, but they took care of me by hosting two book signing events and allowing me to have a display in the Fairfield Civic Center branch. While having my book on the shelves in Barnes & Noble and online on Amazon was cool, I knew I had arrived when it was available in the library that I have been going to for over forty-five years.

I so appreciate locals who sold my first book at brick-and-mortar spots, including Lesa Gonzalez of Dave's Giant Hamburgers, Saeb and Nabiha Ziadeh of Joe's Buffet, Joe Neitzel of the Solano History Exploration Center and real-life Marvel superhero John Harter of Waterfront Comics.

I do want to offer sincere apologies to Aileen Butt and the family of Elsie Nakamura for misspelling their names in my first book. Oh, and I apologize in advance to anyone who was hoping that the pictures in this book would be scratch and sniff. You will have to use your memory and imagination instead.

What this project required that my first did not was to conduct a lot of new interviews. I am so thankful for the insights offered by Art Engell, Fairfield Mayor Gary Falati, Nanciann Gregg, Jimmy Harter, John Harter, Jimmy Hung, Mary Ikenaga, Judy A. Johnson, Onis Lentz, Ed Lockhart, Susan Macy Luckenback, Michelle Marquardt, Kirsten McFall, Karen Bennett Moore, Jayne Nakamura, Cathy O'Dell, Blanca Piedra, Claudette Ramirez, David Salvitti, Greta Salvitti, Suisun City Mayor/Solano County Supervisor Jim Spering, Shari Stevens, Gene Thacker, Toni Todd and James Washington.

I have deep and lasting gratitude for the kind and helpful folks at The History Press/Arcadia Publishing for helping me birth and launch my projects.

Special thanks to Sonny Rollins, the Count Basie Orchestra, Chuck Mangione, the Jeff Lorber Fusion and Booker T. & the M.G.'s, whose instrumental jams helped propel my writing.

Now, similar to how I've said my first book was certainly never meant to be the *Encyclopedia Fairfieldica*, this book is not meant to cover every last restaurant that has ever called Fairfield home.

I just hope to give y'all, well, a taste.

1

The Earliest Fairfield Eateries

I'm afraid I am a bit of a technophobe—a nineteenth-century man caught in the twenty-first century. But there is one piece of technology that I would especially welcome: a device to automatically balance restaurant tables on all four legs so that they don't rock back and forth.
—American physicist Leonard Susskind

efore we get to the hyperlocal focus of this book, let's take a macro view of restaurants for a moment. According to the book *The Restaurant: From Concept to Operation* by John R. Walker, the earliest known example of a restaurant dates to 512 BCE in ancient Egypt, and the menu was rather limited. In fact, it brings to mind the movie *My Cousin Vinny*, in which the title character and his fiancée go to a southern diner and look over the menu that lists only "breakfast, lunch and dinner." The ancient Egyptian eatery was even more Spartan, as it served just one dish that consisted of cereal, wild fowl and onion. I can't help but wonder if the servers had to announce it to patrons every day as the special.

The ancient Romans loved to get their grub on, and the proof can be found in the Roman town Herculaneum near Naples. It was frozen in time by tons of mud and lava when Mount Vesuvius erupted in 60 CE. They had taverns, snack bars and bakeries—they even had several restaurants that were almost identical to each other, strongly suggesting that the idea of franchising isn't exactly a modern-day concept.

UNION AVE. LOOKING SOUTH FAIRFIELD CAL.

Union Avenue in the early 1900s. *Tim Farmer collection.*

The oldest American restaurant (not continuously running as such but founded many years ago) is the White Horse Tavern in Newport, Rhode Island, which was constructed before 1673. What its original colonial menu included is not clear, but today, it is hoity-toity, featuring items like crispy pork belly, Scotch duck eggs, escargot, seared foie gras and roasted bone marrow.

The oldest restaurant in California is the Tadich Grill, which was established in 1849 by Croatian immigrants in San Francisco.

Meanwhile, back in Fairfield, California in the late summer of 1903, a group of civic volunteers called the Fairfield Improvement Club met in the superior courtroom to discuss forming a sanitary district to install a much-needed sewer system in the town. However, after much discussion, they decided to go big or go home and take a vote from the citizenry about incorporating or becoming a city. That way, they could tackle a number of issues simultaneously for the small but steadily growing farm community instead of facing them piecemeal.

A petition was created, and as the law demanded, 50 qualified electors residing within the limits of the proposed corporation attached their signatures to it. Lower taxes, protection against fires, the construction of sidewalks and road repairs were some of the benefits citizens could enjoy from passage of the proposal. A special election was held on December 5,

Solano Street RESTAURANT

—AND—

Tamale Parlors

Meals Served at all hours
Oysters, Tamales and all
Short Orders ....

Everything New
Excellent Appointments
and Good Service

Tamales ordered by 'phone delivered
to your home

JOE CARRILLO

PROPRIETOR

Phone Main 48   Suisun, Cal.

A Solano Street Restaurant advertisement from 1906. *Fairfield Civic Center Library microfilm.*

1903, and of the 130 people who voted, 77 were for and 53 were against the proposal. The city of Fairfield, California, was born.

Interestingly, there is no mention in the existing contemporaneous records of any group of Fairfielders either holding planning meetings beforehand or celebratory dinners after the measure passed at any local restaurants. That's because there really weren't any. Fairfield had been the county seat since 1858, but at the turn of the century, it was still small potatoes compared to its bustling port town neighbor Suisun City. While it may have been the governmental center of Solano County, it was nowhere near being its culinary center.

In perusing period microfilm from 1903, I found that the Arlington Hotel in Suisun had the Grill Room, which was open from 7:30 p.m. to 1:00 a.m. and featured oysters and short orders served "in first-class style." Down the road a bit, Vacaville had the Elite Bar and Grill Room, which boasted "only the choicest liquors, wines, beers and leading brands of cigars." The meals there were "for travelling men" and were served to order at all hours. They included the choicest meats, game, poultry, oysters, fruit and pastries.

In its fledgling days as a city, local Fairfield folks evidently didn't eat in restaurants that often but prepared and ate meals at home. The various ingredients for their repasts could usually be found in Suisun City, like the Pioneer Meat Market on Main Street. It was a wholesale and retail dealer of cattle, sheep and hogs and sold fresh and salted meats, hams, bacon and lard. Another Suisun store, J.C. Murphy, sold fruit, vegetables and canned goods, plus coffees and teas.

The closest thing to a restaurant in Fairfield at that time (or at least the closest thing to a restaurant that bought advertising in the local newspaper) was the Gem Candy Store. It was owned by a Mrs. Hattie Carpenter and featured candies, nuts, tropical fruits, teas, coffees, fresh bread and several nonfood items, like stationery and sewing accoutrements.

In 1906, the Solano Street Restaurant and Tamale Parlor in Suisun City served meals at all hours and predated Uber Eats and DoorDash by over a century by offering "tamales ordered by phone delivered to your home." That same year, a Suisun City eatery owned by John Loez offered fresh oysters, crabs, chicken tamales, bread, pies and cakes, all made on the premises. The advertisement listed the establishment's selling points as "cheap prices," "everything good" and "separate rooms for ladies." Wait—what? Why is that a selling point? So they didn't have to see how men eat?

In the late 1920s, there is mention of a place located on Texas and Taylor Streets called the De Luxe Restaurant and a reference to the popular Palace Grill, which was located at 825 Texas Street. (In 2022, it is called the Million Thai Restaurant.)

Proprietor John Philes, who owned the Plaza Grill in Suisun City, offered waffles at all hours that were evidently served with a side order of racism. An advertisement in the 1925 Armijo High School *La Mezcla* yearbook touted his "All White Help."

In 1927, Bandana Lou's opened on Rockville Road, and folks gathered there to savor the restaurant's fried chicken and to kick up their heels to the sounds of live bands on the upstairs dance floor. The crumbling remains of Bandana Lou's are still present in 2022, as it later became the Iwama Market.

The Campbell's Café opened for business in 1939. It was located across the street from where Armijo High's gym was built a few years later on the side that faces North Texas Street. It was the first in a long series of restaurants in that location that served generations of Armijo High students until the late 1980s.

YOZO IKENAGA AND THE PARK INN

On July 25, 1907, Yozo Ikenaga landed with his father, Naozo, at the port in Seattle, Washington. They had come from Hyōgo, Japan, to stay with Naozo's brother in San Francisco. When he arrived in the United States, Yozo was a four-foot-seven-inch thirteen-year-old with fifty dollars in his pocket. By 1917, he was the owner of the Mint Restaurant in Suisun City on Main Street. He'd come to work with his uncle and bought the business when his uncle went back to Japan. At that time, it was a candy store and ice cream parlor.

In November 1927, members of the Suisun Lions Club, along with local teachers and others, were the guests of Yozo Ikenaga at the soft opening of his expansion of the Mint into the Mint Grill. The annex to the establishment was to be used for banquets, private parties and such, and a phonograph

Suisun City restauranteur Yozo Ikenaga, who owned and operated the Mint Grill and the Park Inn. *Courtesy of Mary Ikenaga.*

was installed so dance music could be played anytime someone wanted to get their groove on. There was a twenty-by-forty-foot hardwood dance floor in the back of the building.

Several local businesses sent well-wishes on Ikenaga's new venture.

"The array of flowers about the place in the form of wreaths, horseshoes, bouquets, sprays and potted plants well told of the popularity in which the host is held," a newspaper account of the affair stated.

There were brief remarks about the history of Thanksgiving by the president of the club and then a Miss Emily Reese accompanied by Miss Anna Kyle rendered a "delightful duet," followed by another with Reese and K.I. Jones.

Yozo Ikenaga made the following statement that was read aloud by another member:

Club president, fellow Lions and ladies: your joy in being here is no greater than mine in having you all as my guests. I deeply and truly enjoy being a Lion and especially a member of the Suisun Den, and I feel that it is only right to have my fellow Lions feasting with me on this, the opening night of our new banquet hall. You are all royally welcome, and I trust that whenever your hunting is poor that you will remember my welcome and drop into my den and eat with me. The reason for the opening of this new room is to provide Suisun with the finest kind of a place, where you will feel like coming and bringing your family to enjoy your meals in a homelike place. Again, bidding you all welcome and wishing the Lions Club all success. I am more than glad to be the Lion host on this occasion.

After the soft opening, the Mint Grill opened to the public the following evening and featured a six-course turkey dinner. Yozo Ikenaga's standing in the local community was rock solid, and four years later, he was elected president of the Suisun Fishing Club.

With his wife, Tsuyako, Yozo had four children: Namiko, Frank, George and Mary. The baby of the family, Mary Ikenaga, who in 2022 is ninety-three and living in San Francisco, remembered her father:

I think we were the only Japanese family that lived in the city of Suisun. All of the others lived in the Suisun Valley and were farmers. We lived near [local lawyer and California state assemblyman] *Ernest Crowley. I was my father's pet. Whenever I wanted ice cream, I could have it. Sometimes, even when he was just going to put the car in the garage, he would call me, and I would come running out there and get in the car with him and we would drive into the garage* [laughs].

When it came to pastimes, besides fishing in the Suisun Slough on his boat, Yozo was also a camera enthusiast and an in-demand budding cinematographer. He would break out his projector and show reels of interesting local events he had captured to rapt members of Suisun City and Fairfield service clubs. A 1930 *Napa Journal* newspaper article detailed one such meeting, where Ikenaga held forth, showing "moving pictures" of the Chief Solano Pageant, Boy and Girl Scouts, an airplane flight in Sacramento and the devastating 1929 fire that started in the county library that was then housed inside the old Armijo High School building on Union Avenue.

In 1929, an incident Yozo Ikenaga experienced was so unusual that it made its way into the Associated Press and was thus printed in Oakland and Modesto, California newspapers as well as newspapers in Eugene, Oregon, and Boise, Idaho, among others. Ikenaga opened a tin labeled "Florida Grapefruit," and instead of fruit, he found a woman's handkerchief with $1.95 (over $32.00 in 2022) tucked into a corner.

Eleven years later, an article in the August 1, 1940 edition of the *Solano Republican* newspaper featured a headline that read: "American-Born Japanese Purchase Highway Site for New Restaurant." The American-born Japanese buyers were Jimmy and Namiko Ikenaga. They bought eight and a half acres south of Highway 40 and one and a half miles west of the courthouse from Mrs. Rutherford Chadbourne.

Jimmy and Namiko had signed the dotted lines, but the operator and face of the new venture was their brother and father, respectively, Yozo Ikenaga. The California Alien Land Law of 1913 prohibited "aliens ineligible for citizenship," like Yozo, a Japanese national, from owning agricultural land or possessing long-term leases over it.

The new place was to be called the Park Inn and would cater to Fairfielders and take advantage of road-weary, hungry motorists traveling east and west down U.S. Highway 40. The newspaper announcement said the restaurant would specialize in chicken dinners and broiled, grilled and planked steaks and would host private parties, banquets and other special

PHONE 94-F-21 OPEN A. M. TO P. M.

Park Inn

The Log Cabin Building
1 1-2 MILES WEST OF FAIRFIELD
ON HIGHWAY 40

SPECIAL ATTENTION GIVEN TO BANQUETS
WE SPECIALIZE IN CHARCOAL BROILING
YOZO IKENAGA, PROP.
P. O. BOX 252, SUISUN, CAL.

● WE HAVE SERVED THIS COMMUNITY FOR THE PAST 29 YEARS ●
FORMERLY

A vintage Park Inn "Log Cabin Building" business card. *Courtesy of Mary Ikenaga.*

occasions. Freshness was guaranteed, as the chickens and other fowl, as well as all vegetables, would be grown at the site.

The Ikenagas' stated goal was for the new restaurant to be the finest resort in Solano County, equal in attractiveness to any along the highway between the bay district and the Oregon border.

A few months after the initial announcement, Yozo Ikenaga closed the doors of the Mint Grill and moved its refrigeration plant, large steel range and other equipment to the new family venture.

The Park Inn had its grand opening on November 3, 1940, and more than 250 people helped christen the new spot. The dinner was comprised of turkey and grilled steaks, sides of mashed potatoes, fresh vegetables, and for dessert, there was apple pie à la mode or a pineapple sundae. Little Mary Ikenaga wore a kimono and greeted customers.

A fourteen-foot-tall neon sign with three-foot-tall letters spelling out "EAT" could be seen for more than half a mile, and if that wasn't enough, two floodlights helped inaugural eaters find their way.

The main building was described as large and rustic and was set seventy-five feet away from the highway. A vintage business card described it as "the log cabin building." It was thirty-four feet wide and one hundred feet long and had a banquet room and dance hall that could accommodate one hundred patrons.

The Park Inn was a runaway hit from the get-go and soon was hosting events like a California Highway Patrol dinner and twenty-five-year Armijo principal James Brownlee's retirement party. In January 1941, the Ikenagas leased the banquet room to Ernest Hickey of Fairfield's Hickey's Brass Rail and Sterling Robinson of Suisun City's Sterling's Tavern, who, as copartners, operated a nightclub inside the restaurant.

Left: An advertisement for the grand opening of Yozo Ikenaga's Park Inn in 1940. *Fairfield Civic Center Library microfilm.*

Below: The Park Inn, which later became the site of the Black Swan and the Ranch House. *Courtesy of Mary Ikenaga.*

Business was booming, but it came to a screeching halt on December 7, 1941.

The deadly surprise attack by the Empire of Japan on U.S. forces in Pearl Harbor simultaneously catapulted America into World War II and created fierce anti-Japanese sentiments. Overnight, businesses owned by Americans of Japanese descent were shunned. Those sentiments were given the force of law in the spring of 1942, when President Franklin Roosevelt signed Executive Order 9066, which authorized the secretary of war to prescribe parts of the United States as military zones and to exclude "certain" residents from them.

By the time the order was signed, the Park Inn had already announced its new ownership in January 1941.

Since he was a Japanese national, Yozo was arrested by the FBI and sent to the Poston Internment Camp in Yuma County, Arizona. The rest of his family was sent to a camp in Gila, Arizona. The longtime restaurateur who always insisted on meticulous attention to detail to make sure his customers felt at home and comfortable was subjected to 115° Fahrenheit days and nights in which the temperatures got as low as 35° Fahrenheit. Diseases like tuberculosis ran roughshod over the Poston detainees.

On January 20, 1944, Yozo Ikenaga died at a hospital near the internment camp; cancer had spread to many of his major organs. He had been released to his family, and they surrounded him on his death bed. His brother Jimmy had been granted leave from the United States Army, in which he served as a technician, fifth grade, with the all-Japanese-American 442nd Regimental Combat Team, one of the most decorated units in the war. He was briefly allowed to stop fighting for the country that had imprisoned his entire family, including his dying brother.

On Yozo Ikenaga's death certificate, his usual occupation was noted as the proprietor of the Park Inn. The restaurant lived on, albeit changed.

THE BLACK SWAN, LIKE A PHOENIX, IS BORN

Many factors go into making a restaurant successful—location, good food and service, reasonable prices and an inviting atmosphere are among them. A memorable name helps as well.

In 1943, James and Frances Dalkas, who had previously owned the Palace Grill, came up with a unique way to name their new business venture: they held a contest. More than fifty suggested names for their new restaurant were submitted, and the winner was sent in by Mrs. Helen Weir, the assistant cashier at the Solano County Bank and the wife of David Weir, the publisher of the *Solano Republican* newspaper. She received a one-hundred-dollar savings bond.

The winning entry was the Black Swan.

Now, the naming was more of a rebranding than merely a naming. You see, the establishment the Dalkases were taking over was the former Park Inn.

The aforementioned *Solano Republican* newspaper, which had gushed about Yozo Ikenaga and the Park Inn a few years prior, cynically

Above: The exterior of the Black Swan, which had once housed the Park Inn. *Tim Farmer collection.*

Left: A 1951 advertisement for the Black Swan's specialties: the "King-Sized Hamburger" and the "Queen of Tarts." *Fairfield Civic Center Library microfilm.*

announced the name change in this way: "The Inn, formerly owned by Yozo Ikenaga, now in an internment center for unworthy Japs, is being thoroughly restored and redecorated and will be formally opened as soon as the new furniture arrives from the east."

One of the distinct features of the restaurant was a pair of signs featuring a huge namesake ebony aquatic bird.

The grand opening took place on Sunday, December 12, 1943. The Dalkases ran the Black Swan for four years, and then in April 1947, they took out a sizeable advertisement in the newspaper, thanking the public for their patronage and announcing the new owners: Mrs. Adele Buzzini, Mr. and Mrs. Arnold Maupin and Mr. and Mrs. Otto Zinke. The group had owned and operated the Buckhorn in Dixon for seven years and brought their experience to the new place.

The new owners gave the restaurant a facelift and added a modern and well-stocked cocktail lounge. The grand reopening was held on April 15, 1947, and an estimated seven hundred to eight hundred people visited throughout the day. In 1956, the Maupins sold the place and opened Arnold's Food, a burger joint off Highway 40. The familiar Black Swan signs remained for years after the restaurant had drifted into memory. In 1963, the spot became a hofbräu called the Ranch House owned by Brazilian Jose "The South American Kid" Feitor. Eventually, the building was destroyed in a fire.

The Black Swan has the distinction of being one of the oldest former restaurants that some locals still recall.

Sharon Maupin Tonnesen: My mom and dad bought the Black Swan when I was twelve years old. My brother Dave and my sister Claudia and I all worked and lived there for the next six years. We also entertained for the banquets and parties. My mom played the organ, and we sang. The hat was always passed, and we made lots of money.

Barbara Barnes Green: My parents and I ate at the Black Swan occasionally. I used to twirl on those pedestal seats at the counter.

Steve Keiser: My mom and dad used to go there, but they called it the Dirty Duck!

POSTWAR FAIRFIELD BOOMS

The addition of the Fairfield-Suisun Army Air Base (later known as Travis Air Force Base) in 1942 fueled a boom in the Fairfield economy, and in the early postwar era, the county seat began to sprout new businesses left and right. As the city grew and residents had more disposable income, restaurants followed. Traffic on U.S. Highway 40 increased, and since cars rumbled down through the heart of the city, eateries sprang up to cater to them as well as hungry locals.

On Halloween in 1946, the Campos Food Fair, owned by future Fairfield mayor Manuel Campos, opened its doors at 735 Texas Street for the first time. Harry Theissen opened a sprawling Fairfield Feed Store on Union Avenue, which, decades later, would morph into Theissen's Pet Store. The following year, Gillespie Cleaners moved from its Jackson Street space to a two-story building on the corner of Pennsylvania and Texas Streets that had a fur vault. The building has now been home to the *Daily Republic* since 1961.

The following is a look at a few of the numerous eateries that were established in Fairfield in the years immediately following the cessation of hostilities in World War II.

THE OCTO INN: HOW DOES A RESTAURANT BECOME A SOCCER COMPLEX?

Around 1935, Onis James Lentz and his wife, Ida May, opened the Octo Inn near what in 2022 is the corner of West Texas Street and Beck Avenue. They also owned approximately twenty-five to thirty acres of property in the area.

Longtime Fairfield businessman Art Engell, who graduated from Armijo High School with the class of 1949, remembered the Lentz family and the restaurant: "Their grandson was a year younger than me. It was called the Octo-Inn because it was an eight-sided building. It was a restaurant and a gas station."

In 2021, Onis Charles Lentz, named after his grandfather, was living in Merced and was still active with the Boy Scouts after eighty years. He shared remembrances of his family's restaurant. "Why they built it with eight sides, I have no idea. It had a gas station outside with those now-old-fashioned pumps, and inside were booths for seating, and at one end was a kitchen; the other side was a bar. It was built of stucco with a dull yellow color and had red trim with a big wooden sign. Their house next door was the same color."

Above: The oft-robbed eight-sided Octo Inn. *Armijo High yearbook, 1953.*

Right: A 1948 *Solano Republican* newspaper article about one of the many Octo Inn burglaries. *Fairfield Civic Center Library microfilm.*

Octo Inn Burglars Plead Guilty Here

Robert Anderson, 27, and Pershing Hermmerd, 26, both ex-convicts, pleaded guilty to a charge of burglary of Octo Inn on Highway 40, west of Fairfield on the morning of May 3 and will be sentenced by Superior Judge Joseph M. Raines this afternoon (Thursday). As one of the men, Anderson, was armed, the court determined the burglary to be first degree.

The pair was arrested in Octo Inn by Deputy Sheriffs Jule O. Pritchard, George Warren and Stanley Emerson after they set off a burglar alarm when they forced the front door of the service station and cafe. Tear gas was used by the officers in forcing the men from the inn.

While hamburgers and homemade pies were the restaurant's specialties, the Octo Inn became known more for being a magnet for burglars. That was probably due to its then relatively isolated location away from the heart of Fairfield and close to the getaway route of U.S. Highway 40. A January 1954 newspaper article stated that the Octo Inn had been burglarized twenty times in nineteen years. Former Solano County undersheriff Stanley Emerson was with the department from 1946 to 1980, and at the age of one hundred in 2019 still had razor-sharp memories about all the break-ins.

> *It was the perfect spot to commit burglary, but we caught all of them. I even drilled a hole in the wall, so if someone tried to hole up in the bathroom, I could shoot some tear gas in there. We put mirrors behind the bar so you could see if someone was crouched back there hiding, and that got a few. It got to the point where I would go to San Quentin with a prisoner, and they would say, "Is this another Octo Inn deal?"*

Eventually, Onis J. Lentz sold the restaurant to Myron Ulshoffer, his wife's brother, in the 1940s. Ulshoffer had his own run-ins with burglars and installed an alarm system in the restaurant that would alert him at his house. In May 1945, three youths broke in around 6:00 a.m. and Ulshoffer came running with his shotgun. One of the young thieves took two shots at the owner but missed, and Ulshoffer opened fire. Four days later, the thieves made their appearance in Judge Georgia Crowley's courtroom, one of them on a stretcher after being hit by the shotgun blast in his head and torso. The trio became another "Octo Inn deal."

Ulshoffer and his wife, Dorothy, ran the Octo Inn for some time but eventually tore it down and built a motel near what is now the Interstate 80 West exit for Oliver Road. Called the My and Dot Motel, it served travelers on the highway and was far enough away from Fairfield proper that it was also a popular trysting spot—the local "no-tell motel"—before Sleepy Hollow down the road later claimed that title.

While memories of the old restaurant have faded away, the name Octo Inn lives on in Fairfield. The land became the Octo Inn Retention Basin, used to manage storm water runoff to prevent flooding and downstream erosion. Then after a concerted effort to provide more exercise facilities for Fairfield youth, the city entered into an agreement with the Fairfield Youth Soccer League. The forty-acre site, which had previously been purchased by the city, had its grand opening on October 4, 1997, as the Octo Inn Soccer Complex.

RISE OF THE FOUNTAINS AND CAFÉS

In the modern era, soda fountains have become the place where customers can top off their soft drinks by pressing their cup against a lever that dispenses the syrup and carbonated water beverage. But back in the day, fountains were a whole genre of eatery. U.S. physician Samuel Fahnestock was awarded the first soda fountain patent in 1819. His invention was a device that was hidden under a counter that was shaped like a barrel and dispensed carbonated water with a pump or spigot.

Fertilizing the explosion of local fountains was the trifecta of the air force base, the traffic down Highway 40 and baby boomers with disposable income becoming teenagers. The local fountains had all manner of toppings for ice cream sundaes, as well as different syrups to dress up Coca-Cola, including cherry, lemon and even chocolate. Jukeboxes with swing, pop, R&B and rock and roll records became the centerpiece of numerous local fountains.

In addition to the ones highlighted in the following sections, they also included the Fairfield Fountain, Suisun Ice and Soda Works, the Fruit Bowl Café on Highway 40, Top Notch Coffee Shop on Main Street in Suisun City and the C.&K. Drive-In, which was located on Union Avenue near where the twin cities used to meet before they were separated by the Highway 12 overpass in 1984.

Horgan's

In January 1938, Dennis and Laura Horgan moved from Vallejo to Empire Street in Fairfield and purchased a soda fountain, which was located in the old theater building on the corner of Jackson and Texas Streets. Dennis Horgan was no stranger to the area, as he had been a delivery man for Golden State Ice Cream in Fairfield for fifteen years prior to becoming a shop owner.

Horgan's soon became a social hub for young people, as it was close to the Solano Theatre. Allan Witt's barbershop was next door, and some of his customers would go to Horgan's for ice cream while waiting to get their hair cut.

According to former Fairfielder Susan Macy Luckenback, the granddaughter of the Horgans, the soda fountain's specialty was extra-thick milkshakes. While there are some even today who complain about burger joints like Dave's Giant Hamburgers that don't serve French fries, back in the

The Solano Theatre on the corner of Jackson and Texas Streets. In the 1930s, Horgan's and other fountains called that corner home. *Tim Farmer collection.*

late 1930s, fries were reserved for only the finest restaurants. When it came to accompanying burgers, potato chips usually rode shotgun.

While Horgan's was only in existence a brief three years and there aren't too many folks still living who are old enough to remember it, Luckenback related that some Fairfielders do have a one-degree-of-separation link to the 1930s business owners. The Red Top Dairy and Restaurant used her grandmother Horgan's pasta sauce recipe for years.

Airline Coffee Shop and Restaurant

The Airline Coffee Shop and Restaurant (or Airline Café) opened its doors at 844 Texas Street for the first time in February 1946. The original owners were Miguel Morilla and Bert and Manuel Reguera (who were later the original owners of the Corner Variety Store). They offered complete lunches and dinners, fountain service and sandwiches with table service in comfortable booths. Evidently, they were not in it for the long haul, as they sold the restaurant to two new managers, Mike Gabilan and Frank Mellado, in October of that year. The new team literally had roots in the area, as they were also orchard owners in Suisun Valley.

The Airline Café downtown in 1963. *Courtesy of Timothy Ryan.*

However, roots or no, by March of the following year, the restaurant had been sold yet again, this time to Frank and Eugina Andronis.

The Airline Coffee Shop was open every day of the week, and its advertisements emphasized not letting "mother slave over the family's dinners." One advertisement included the following: "Our home-style dinners are a treat for every member of the family. Mother enjoys the rest.... Dad enjoys the economy, and everybody enjoys the delicious variety of foods tastily prepared by Frank Andronis, the chef, himself."

The advertisement was signed: "YOUR HOSTS AND OLD FAIRFIELD FRIENDS, MR. & MRS. FRANK ANDRONIS."

The menu included minestrone soup, Italian dinners, grilled lamb chops, fried spring chicken, veal scaloppini, potatoes, vegetables and ice cream.

Numerous old-time Fairfielders recall the Andronises' Airline Café period, with many incorrectly assuming they were the original owners.

Flo Masani: I remember the Airline Café! A favorite hangout for kids in the '50s! Burgers, fries and flavored fountain Cokes! Good times listening to juke box music and flirting with the boys!

Gloria Jean Lee: We used to eat there twice a month after church. We loved the hot roast beef sandwiches and hamburgers! We would eat, then we'd window shop and go home.

Susan Macy Luckenbach: I wasn't a fan. I had pancakes there in the '50s that tasted like metal.

Keith Hayes: I ran around with the owners' son Pete Andronis from 1947 until he moved to Texas. He passed away in 2000. I remember when we were young boys, Pete would lift up the seat cushions after closing time, looking for change that had fallen out of customers' pockets. Sometimes, he found several dollars—a lot of money then. Pete's father always had a wad of cash, and some people used to call him "Money Bags." I remember December 4, 1952, which was Pete's birthday, and Mr. Andronis pulled out a wad of money, peeled off one hundred dollars and gave it to Pete and said, "Happy birthday." At the time, that was more money than I had ever seen at one time.

While the Andronis family were of Greek descent, the food they served at the Airline Café did not reflect their heritage; it was typical American lunch/dinner fare. They eventually sold the business to Vaughn L. Dudley Jr. and his wife, Lotte. Lotte was born and raised in Munich, Germany, and they added authentic Deutschland dishes to the menu, including wiener schnitzel, smoked goulash and pork chops with sauerkraut.

Lotte had met and married then Airman Dudley in 1955, and they moved to Fairfield in 1960. Lotte's son from a previous relationship, Heinz Ruchti, stowed away on a ship until he was discovered. Then Lotte flew to New York and brought him back with her to Fairfield. Heinz attended Armijo High, where he tried to fit in despite the language barrier.

On December 21, 1967, Heinz enlisted in the U.S. Marine Corps and soon afterward received orders for duty in Vietnam. Tragically, on September 11, 1967, he was killed by fragmentation wounds from hostile artillery fire and received a posthumous Purple Heart Medal. Private First-Class Heinz Ruchti is honored on 44W, line 29 of the Vietnam Veterans Memorial Wall.

Dale Metoxen: I remember Heinz and his family. My twin brother and I were only ten years old, and Heinz would give us free cokes when we saw him. I remember the day we found out Heinz died and went to see his mother Lotte in tears. I have an etching from the Vietnam memorial in Sacramento.

Bill Boyce: It broke my heart when I heard Heinz lost his life in Vietnam. Me, Jim Perez and Heinz went on an overnight camping/fishing trip to Lake Berryessa once. What a great time we had, and Jim caught a largemouth bass. A day or two prior, the three of us were walking past the old jailhouse on Empire Street when Heinz spotted graffiti, the word "F——." He asked Jim what that word was and proceeded to pronounce it "fuke." We had a great laugh and explained the correct way to say it and its meaning. Little things you take for granted and never know how that moment is forever etched in your brain, especially when a local and one of our own is taken way before their time. I am still saddened by his loss. He was just a really pleasant guy, still learning the English language, fitting in and trying to learn the culture. Rest in peace, my friend.

Loren's Fountain

Although there were numerous fountain-type shops and ice cream joints in both Fairfield and Suisun City, only one could claim to have the absolute largest ice cream cone, and that was Loren's Fountain. It was not the actual cones they served but the huge one on the sign hanging in front the shop, which used to be located at 801 Texas Street.

Before it became Loren's Fountain, it had a go as Chester's Creamery and Chester's Fountain in the 1940s. Back then, the sign featured what appeared to be a giant sundae. Its claim to fame was that its ice cream was made right in front of the customers' eyes.

The namesake owner of Loren's Fountain was Loren Bailey who ran the shop from 1942 to 1955, when he sold it to Bernard and Marjorie Bornstein. Years later, the Bornstein's daughter Lori Lorenz and her now-ex-husband ran a consignment store in downtown Fairfield called the Treasure Chest. Through imagination and artistic license, Lorenz merged the memories of

A photograph of the painting of Loren's Fountain and the Treasure Chest by artist Donna Covey that was commissioned by Lori Lorenz. *Courtesy of Lori Lorenz.*

the two businesses when she commissioned a painting by artist Donna Covey to show them across Texas Street from each other.

Other locals shared memories of Loren's Fountain on Facebook:

> *Frema Byrd: As an Armijo Freshman in 1958–59, the last year the old Armijo building on Union Avenue was used, I went there every day for lunch, as there was no cafeteria yet on the new campus. Next stop was the bakery for a cream puff that went back to science class with me. Mr. Federoff nailed me when he saw powdered sugar on my mouth. I learned eating in class was not allowed.*

> *JoAnn Hinkson Beebe: French fries and cherry coke…the lunch of champions.*

> *Abe Bautista: One of the places I really liked downtown was Loren's Fountain; it was just like* Happy Days—*ice cream, soda jerks, kids listening to music. They wouldn't let me in because I was still young…but I would sneak in!*

Red Top Fountain

In 1945, Leo McInnis, the namesake for the "McInnis Corner" on the clock that, in 2022, sits above the corner of Jefferson and Texas Streets downtown, leased that location to Albert Ferrari, who five years earlier had founded Red Top Dairy in Vallejo. The location had previously been Joe Serpas's O.K. Sweet Shop and a Greyhound bus depot. Ferrari converted it into a modern fountain and lunch plate spot.

The grand opening of Red Top Fountain was held on February 23, 1946. It offered complete fountain service with twenty-five stools, and in addition to "extra rich, pure ice cream containing 16 percent butterfat," the shop sold sandwiches, soups, chili and other items. The original manager was Pat Patterson, but by August 1, new owners/managers Francis J. Higgins and Morgan L. Hannigan took over the venture.

Morgan Hannigan was nicknamed "Morgue" not only because it was a homonym for the shortened form of his first name, but because he was also the deputy county coroner. Red Top Fountain was a popular spot with the Armijo High lunch crowd, county workers and motorists headed east or west on U.S. Highway 40.

The restaurant was first known as Red Top Fountain, then H.&H. Fountain after the owners' initials, and then, in 1950, Hannigan bought out Higgins and it became Hannigan's Fountain.

The O.K. Sweet Shop, which used to be on the corner of Jefferson Street and North Texas Street where the Red Top Fountain was later located. *Courtesy of Art Engell.*

Hannigan's Fountain was packed with Armijo students before school, after school and especially at lunch time. *Armijo High yearbook, 1956.*

It wasn't just about banana splits, jukeboxes and cherry cokes, however. Hannigan's was kitty-corner to the old USO building, which closed in December 1947. The Suisun Airman's Club opened in 1948 to fill the void but closed two years later. In 1951, a volunteer-led serviceman's information booth opened at Hannigan's to assist servicemen with information regarding housing, places of amusement, transportation, religious organizations and other needs.

Dot Danielson Little: I worked at Red Top Fountain mostly on weekends, summers and holidays, from the ages of sixteen to eighteen back in 1953 to 1955. Morgan and his wife, Jeanne, were wonderful people and fun to work for. Many people from the Solano County Courthouse would lunch at Hannigan's, and Morgan was always kidding with them. Morgan had the reputation of making his hamburgers so thin that you could see through them. There was a door that went to a small cubby that went from the fountain to Mac's Bar next door. I often saw food go through there but never saw drinks come back through. I babysat Morgan and Jeanne's sons, Tom and Pat, and their mom often said I was more of a referee than a babysitter.

Thomas M. Hannigan worked at his dad's shop, first washing dishes for seventy cents an hour and then short order cooking the hamburgers and other fare. "Fairfield was very small when we moved there, I think the population might have been 2,800. The only paved street curb to curb was Texas Street," Hannigan said in 2016. "Missouri Street to the south and Empire Street to the north were paved in the middle, but the rest of the street to the curb was gravel."

Hannigan had neighborhood friends whom he attended grammar school with, played sports with in loosely organized city leagues and worked with in the summertime. He intended to attend Armijo High School with them when the 1954 school year began in September. However, on May 11, 1954, the Armijo Union High School student body made nationwide news when students staged an impromptu strike. The walkout was to protest the firing of two popular staff members.

Red Top Fountain was a block away from the school, so Morgan Hannigan saw the whole thing unfold and decided his son would not be going to that school. Instead, Thomas Hannigan took the Greyhound bus from the depot next door to the shop to Vallejo each morning, where he attended co-ed St. Vincent's Catholic school. Originally, he attended under protest, but he came to like the school a lot. "I actually got in more trouble at St. Vincent's than I ever would have at Armijo," Hannigan said. That trouble did not prevent the former Red Top Fountain dishwasher from later becoming a Fairfield city councilman, mayor, Solano County supervisor and California State assemblyman.

2
Burger Joints and Other Fast Food

I like my shame straight-up and honest, and nobody does it better than In-N-Out Burger. You go to In-N-Out Burger, and they ask you the most shameful question in fast food. "I'll have a burger, fries and a Coke." "Will you be eating in the car?" "Yeah. I think so."
—American comedian Tom Segura

In *Growing Up in Fairfield, California*, I included a Fairfield fast-food timeline that gave an overview of quick and easy eateries that have existed in the county seat over the years. This is not meant to replicate that; instead, it will delve a little deeper and flesh out the previously published outline. Oh, and it is not meant to be exhaustive either.

There were numerous early places that served hamburgers, but their heydays and when they started to pick up steam was definitely in the 1950s. Lifelong Fairfielder Art Engell remembered a restaurant called the Shack around 1939 that, at one time, was part-owned by former Fairfielder Ray Ann Sullivan's father, Ray Fune. Engell remembered that the Shack's ten-cent hamburgers were too big for him to finish as a kid. He also said the establishment later changed hands over a poker game.

SNO-WHITE/SNO-MAN HITS ARMIJO STUDENTS WHERE THEY LIVE

In June 1950, a front-page article in the *Solano Republican* newspaper announced, "Drive-In Ice Cream Plant to Be Built." It evidently was to take

The Sno-White Drive-In, later the Sno-Man Drive-In, stuck in the minds of many Armijo students way longer than algebra ever did. *Armijo High yearbook, 1955.*

the place of a local eyesore. The article said the old James T. Wells house on Union Avenue, said to be one of the oldest homes in Fairfield, would be razed to make room. They evidently turned an eyesore into a sight for sore eyes, as eating at that little hamburger and soft serve ice cream spot is a cherished memory for generations of Armijo High students.

Located at 530 Union Avenue, it was called the Sno-White for about a decade before becoming the Sno-Man.

The Sno-White Company of Lodi ran a chain of restaurants, which, by the mid-1960s, had approximately two hundred locations in California (including one in Vacaville) and two in Guam. Its specialties included the Hi Hat Burger, crinkle-cut fries, malted milkshakes, tacos, foot-long hot dogs, deep-fried burritos and soft serve ice cream, including chocolate-dipped cones.

While it wasn't hit with anywhere near the frequency of the oft-robbed Octo Inn, thieves did try their hands at the Sno-Man as well. In 1956, it was burglarized three times in one week. The first heist netted about $150, the second nothing and the third only about $3, all in pennies.

In 1968, a pair of sixteen-year-olds were caught trying to burglarize the eatery. When police arrived after being tipped off by a motorist, one of the

SNO-MAN DRIVE-INN
(formerly Sno-White)
530 UNION AVENUE.   FAIRFIELD

+ Burgers   + Shakes
+ Hot Dogs

★BUY 'EM
BY THE
SACK

★BUY 'EM
BY THE
SACK

15ᶜ each

AT. & SUN.
. eb. 4th & 5th

CA.. SUN.
Feb. 4th & 5th

UNDER MANAGEMENT OF
PAULINE and **HAROLD ALEXANDER**

OPEN 10:00 A.M. 'til 10:00 P.M.

A Sno-Man Drive-In advertisement from 1961. *Fairfield Civic Center Library microfilm.*

youths ran, but an officer fired a shot in the air and a second one grabbed the would-be thief. At least the first kid could tell other youthful offenders at juvenile hall that he was caught after the cops shot at him. The second burglar was nabbed cowering in the bathroom.

How do you know a restaurant has resonated with the local community? Well, when it opens a sequel just down the road. Sno-Man No. 2, on 1615 West Texas Street (later the home of You's Burgers and the Jelly Donut), opened in the mid-1970s.

Locals recalled the Sno-White/Sno-Man:

Grace Sullivan Chuatakoon: The grilled cheese sandwiches were my favorite there. They used hamburger buns inside out and lots of butter! Mmmmmm!

Lillian Miller: Loved Sno-man. I used to hang out in that little dining room area with my boyfriend. We could make out for hours, and nobody would know because it was so isolated from the kitchen.

Larry Duncan: I loved their foot-long hot dogs and frosties. Thank God I didn't have much money 'cause I sure didn't have any self-control.

Alvin Allen: I was in the fifth grade at Crystal Elementary in 1961 and liked this little girl in my class named Darlene. She and I walked from Suisun to Fairfield for a movie date downtown. While walking back to Suisun, we bought two ice cream cones at the Sno-Man. I was holding mine in my left hand, so I placed my right arm around her shoulders and in doing so, my right hand went right into her ice cream cone. Darlene didn't want it after that, so she gave it to me. I then had two ice cream cones and enjoyed my walk home!

SID'S DRIVE-IN

When many Fairfielders drive by the intersection of North Texas Street and Travis Boulevard, they see the old Heart Federal Savings building, whose large digital clock/thermometer told them what time and temperature it was. But looking through the lens of the mind's eye, many old-timers can still see what used to be in that spot: Sid's Drive-In.

Sid's had an iconic sign with a hamburger and a posing cowgirl on it. According to Sid's waitress Cathy O'Dell, it was originally owned by Sid Withrow, and his little burger fountain restaurant became a hangout for the local teen crowd shortly after it opened in 1955.

Sid's Drive-In was not Withrow's first foray into local dining. He owned the Sno-Man adjacent to Armijo High as well. In March 1955, Sid's Sno-Whites played a benefit basketball game against players from the San Francisco 49ers at the Armijo gym. The 49ers who participated included Hugh McElhenny, Billy Wilson, Bill Johnson, Gorie Soltau, Bob St. Clair and Hardy Brown. The 49ers won by double digits, and the event raised $300 (over $3,000 today), which went toward improving local youth recreation facilities.

Sid's shakes, patty melts, and chili dogs are still recalled more than sixty years later, as is their specialty, the Sid Burger. The secret behind the Sid Burger was not the sauce but how it was cooked. The cooks would cover the burger and buns on the grill with a domed lid, and the grease and grill aroma penetrated the buns to a delicious effect. When the Sid Burger was served, it was topped with an olive on a toothpick.

Maude Arrington later bought Sid's.

Diane Downing McGraugh: If you were the first car there, when you wanted to leave, the car behind you had to move so you could pull out!

A commissioned painting of Sid's Drive-In by artist Donna Covey. *Donna Covey Paintings.*

Gary-Pam DesJardins: Unfortunately, my strongest memory is the night that it burned down. Our whole family walked down to see it.

Tony Horst: Fast hot rods, beehive hairdos, DAs and pegged Levi's.

Debbi Cooper: Sid's was my very first job as a carhop. I loved Maude. She was always such a sweetheart. Her greasy ol' cheeseburgers are still some of the best I've ever had.

Al Cacioppo: My pal "Big Red" Crowder (who was six feet, six inches tall and 285 pounds) and I pulled into a space at Sid's one night next to a '56 Chevy. The passenger was leaning against the inside of the car door talking to the driver. He was smoking a cigarette and casually stuck his arm out the window and flipped the lit butt out without looking. That cig wasn't on Big Red's hood for two seconds before he was dragging the guy out of his window. Holding him by the scruff of his neck and the back of his leather belt, he dangled the guy over the car and suggested he use his lips to get the still lit cig off his hood or suffer the consequences. He lowered the guy down to retrieve it, which he did. Nobody ever messed with Red after that.

HI-FI DRIVE-IN

There are many reasons to frequent a certain burger joint over another—proximity to home, work or school, and whether or not they have a jukebox, parking, certain sides, et cetera. Shoot, it could all come down to a particular burger's secret sauce. The Hi-Fi Drive-In, which used to be located at 1513 West Texas Street, added a different incentive: price. At its grand opening on April 7, 1955, it offered nineteen-cent steak burgers and for the opening week had a special of six for one dollar.

In addition to burgers, hot dogs and fries, Hi-Fi also served fried chicken, Louisiana prawns, fish and chips, barbecued ham, hot fudge or strawberry

The Hi-Fi Drive-In was a popular burger joint and turnaround spot on the weekend Fairfield cruise. *Armijo High yearbook, 1966.*

sundaes, milkshakes and more. During the grand-opening weekend, there was a carousel for the kids, a drawing for a free clock radio and a bicycle, and if a red star appeared on a customer's register receipt, the order was free.

The Hi-Fi Drive-In soon became a teen hangout. Cruising downtown became more of a popular pastime, and many original Fairfield cruisers agreed that Foster's on North Texas Street and the Hi-Fi on West Texas Street were the most popular "turnaround" spots.

In advertisements on its first anniversary, Hi-Fi had a world-famous performer named Homer F. Snow bring his act to perform for Fairfielders three times free of charge in the parking lot of the restaurant. The act included Perry Pelican and Cindi the Sea Lion. As far as can be deduced, it remains the only time a pelican and a sea lion ever performed on West Texas Street.

In 1959, Kern Wiseman, who had owned Kern's Chicken Coop in Stockton, moved to Fairfield with his wife, Lois, and their four children and purchased the Hi-Fi Drive-In. One of the first things he did was raise the price of the steak burgers from nineteen cents to twenty-four cents (which was still a bargain) and reflected it on the neon sign. Other changes were added over the approximately fourteen years that Wiseman owned the eatery; they included many new menu items, such as the Alaskan Giant Burger, fried beef and chicken pies, spaghetti, chili burgers, chili dogs, tacos and tamales. In 1962, Wiseman started a promotion in which customers could save their register receipts, and when they reached $19.95 worth, they could redeem them for five free hamburgers.

In 1970, the first Fairfield McDonald's opened just two and a half miles down the street from Hi-Fi. Its grand opening featured an in-store appearance by who else but Ronald McDonald. But he was not the only burger clown in town. Kern Wiseman would dress up as Dandy the clown, and in 1971, he introduced the Dandy Burger. Microfilm pictures of Dandy have a certain amount of creepiness, but Kern Wiseman's son Doyle told the whole story on Facebook:

My dad was a proud Shriner and, with his friends, entertained kids in the Shriner's hospital. They dressed as clowns. The picture does not do it justice. In person, they were very comical and brought laughter to many sick kids. At the time, I thought my fifty-five-year-old dad was being silly or childish. Now, I am proud that he cared so much and made that commitment while flipping burgers seven days a week.

A 1971 advertisement featuring Hi-Fi Drive-In owner/operator Kern Wiseman as Dandy the Clown. *Fairfield Civic Center Library microfilm.*

Kern Wiseman left the restaurant business in the early '70s, as the explosion of new fast-food places in town were simply too much for the Hi-Fi to compete with. After earning his stripes at Red Carpet Realty, he founded the Wiseman Realty Co., which gave birth to today's Wiseman Company in Fairfield, now run by his son Doyle.

Locals recalled the Hi-Fi Drive In:

> *William A. Bowen: I worked there in 1956, and we frequently peeled and cut (with a machine) one hundred pounds of potatoes for fries each day.*

> *Christy Thompson: I loved the Hi-Fi. When we lived on Fourth Street and I took lessons at the Gina Chappelle Lynch Dance Studio next door, my mom and I would walk there and get soft serve cones after my lessons.*

We'd moved across the freeway by 1971 though, and I'm glad, because if I'd known that clown had ever been a few blocks away, I never would've slept a wink.

Jimmy Spears: Mr. Wiseman was the kindest man. When I came in for a cheeseburger, I never had to tell him how I wanted it. Within minutes, I was out and on my way back to work.

Bill Boyce: I remember the Hi-Fi well. We lived in the hood nearby, Third Street. A friend of mine worked there his senior year of high school. He told me one time he got so busy and overwhelmed trying to get hamburger orders filled, he forgot to put the meat in some of them.

Tragedy struck the Wiseman family twice twenty years apart. In 1986, Don Wiseman died in an accident, and that was prefaced by the death of Doug Wiseman in a car accident in 1966, when he was just a junior at Armijo High School. Doyle Wiseman posted on Facebook about both of his brothers and how much the family misses them. He added a poignant postscript about Doug's sad demise: "His last note to my mom was written on a Hi-Fi order ticket."

A&W DRIVE-IN: ROOT BEER AND THE BURGER FAMILY

The A&W chain of drive-in restaurants, whose name was derived from the initials of founders Roy W. Allen and Frank Wright, started in the 1920s. The fast-food restaurant's claim to fame was delicious root beer served in frosty glass mugs kept in a freezer until filled to order. Once it incorporated and started to sell franchises, it spread like wildfire.

Fairfield's A&W Drive-In had its grand opening on May 16, 1959, near the corner of East Tabor and North Texas Streets. The original owners were Neil and Gerry Gilton. An advertisement touting the event was featured in the *Solano Republican* days before and featured a coupon for ten cents off one gallon of A&W's famous root beer, which brought it down to fifty-five cents. There were free suckers and bubble gum for the kids and a bonus coupon for a free mug of root beer.

Interestingly, the food items touted in the grand-opening advertisement were not burgers but its "famous submarine sandwiches and hot dogs."

Top: A&W Drive-In advertisement. *Courtesy of Karen Bennett Moore.*

Bottom: The A&W Drive-In near the corner of North Texas Street and East Tabor Avenue. *Armijo High yearbook, 1962.*

While it undoubtedly did sell hamburgers, the famous burger family that so many locals remember wasn't introduced until the following year. Boasting that it had a size for every appetite, it featured the Papa Burger (a double patty with all the trimmings), Mama Burger (single patty) and Baby Burger (meat and lettuce).

The Teen Burger was introduced in 1963. There is no evidence in the historical record that it was rebellious, thought it knew everything and

Carinay, Christina and Lida Sarkisian owned and operated the Fairfield A&W in the 1980s. *Fairfield Civic Center Library microfilm.*

screamed at the Mama and Papa Burgers that it hated them for ruining its life, but suspicions remain.

In a January 1964 newspaper advertisement, customers were invited to "try a burger with a delicious mug of root beer and an order of fries." Now, that sentiment didn't change, but the terminology in how to order it did. The cool and correct way to order your Papa Burger with those accompanying items was to say, "I'll have a Papa Burger...in a basket." The burgers were served in little plastic baskets lined with red-checkered, grease-stained deli paper sheets.

As a drive-in with no dine-in facilities, the A&W required customers to park and wait for waitresses to come take their orders and then bring out a tray that hung on the window like a speaker at the Solano Drive-In Theatre down the street. Later, there was a little electronic switch on the signboard menus next to the parking spots that signaled the wait staff.

Advertisements from the '60s touted the restaurant's offerings, like grilled ham and cheese sandwiches, chili dogs, chili burgers, fish sandwiches and more that were all served by the "prettiest carhop service in town." Years later, to keep up with the '80s trends of bigger and better, the restaurant introduced quarter-pound burgers.

Janelle Pritchard Hawkins, who worked at the Fairfield A&W from the late 1950s to early 1960s, shared some remembrances:

> *The baby root beer mugs were the most popular, and everyone wanted them. We always had to make note of how many mugs of each size were on the tray and had to ask people if they "forgot" to return them when we came to pick up the tray. We had to use our tip money to pay for ones customers stole! Being a teenage girl, I really loved that job. I mean, getting to serve all the cute airmen that came in—oh my!*

Another group of men in uniform—Fairfield police officers—always ate at A&W for free when Pritchard worked there.

Ownership of the restaurant changed hands a few times and included the Sarkisian family in the 1980s.

Melissa Greene, Madison Greene and Stanley Greene at A&W on Melissa and Stanley's wedding day in 2019. *Courtesy of Melissa Greene.*

In 1968, Dale and Kathryn Hokanson purchased Foster's Freeze. The Hokansons had moved from Concord, California, and had three children left at home at that time, Garth, Dalene and Reed. What the Hokansons lacked in restaurant experience, they more than made up for with a fierce work ethic and a compelling drive to excel. Garth Hokanson relayed his family's experience in an email in 2021:

All the Hokansons did their part, with my father running the fry side and my mother running the ice cream side. I helped out during daytime rushes but worked the fry side on the evening shifts. Dalene worked both sides as necessary in between her classes at Armijo High School. Reed later became a fry cook, but during his younger years, he cleaned the parking lot, emptied garbage cans and wore the Little Foster ice cream costume on the street to attract customers.

My mother soon became a favorite among the teens, especially girls who would ask if they could talk to her about their problems. She became known as "Big Red" due to her height (five feet, seven inches) and auburn hair. She would sit outside at a table with whoever needed some comfort or a solution to a problem.

Foster's was the "hang-out" place for the teens in Fairfield at that time. After school and evenings, it was always crowded with teenagers socializing with their friends. My father did promotional offers, held special holiday parties and would hire local bands to play in the parking lot on weekends. Business prospered.

My father eventually decided to enclose the front patio of the restaurant to make an indoor dining area. He received approval from the City of Fairfield, and older sons Brent and Lane assisted on the room addition. They were also frequently needed to make repairs on the carport canopy when oversized vehicles would damage the roof. Lane's wife, Pat, also worked as an ice cream server at Foster's.

On one occasion, a man drove up in an old station wagon filled with kids. He came to the window and told my father that he didn't have a cent to his name but had a car full of hungry kids. Minutes later, the kids were enjoying an abundance of hamburgers, French fries and ice cream. These types of stories were common, as my parents were generous people.

After twenty years of profitable business, they sold the franchise but held the second mortgage. The new owners could not make a go out of it, so my family stepped in and reopened it under their leadership again. This happened some years later again, but after that, the business was sold

Left: Kathryn Hokanson, also known as "Big Red," the co-owner of Foster's Old Fashion Freeze with her husband, Dale. *Courtesy of Katerina Uhl.*

Below: Foster's Old Fashion Freeze was a teenage hangout for generations. *Armijo High yearbook, 1966.*

outright. The new owners kept it a short time and closed it down. That was the end of the Foster's Freeze in Fairfield and the years of happy memories so many had there.

While the restaurant is gone—in 2022, it is Yo Sushi—memories remain:

Barry Ainslie: Foster's was the home of the fastest cars in Fairfield.

Ed Lockhart: A buddy and I would sneak out of Mr. Kenny's room at Armijo, and one would go to Dave's for cheeseburgers and the other would go to Foster's for fries and we'd meet back for lunch. Those were the days.

Judy Larcade: I remember going there many evenings (cruising) or for lunch or after school when I attended Armijo High. I remember Karen B. used to wear boxers under her skirts or dresses, and she would bend over and pull her dress over her head and flash the cars as we walked by them on our way up to the window to order! I also remember me catching my hair on fire when trying to light my cigarette, and I was slapping the side of my head trying to put it out.

John Andelfinger: When I was a young lad, I was walking behind Holland Dairy, where construction was going on, and found a wallet in a trench. There was nothing in it except a crisp five-dollar bill. I went directly to Foster's. It was a great day.

Jan Lucas: I worked for Mr. and Mrs. Hokanson, and she was such a doll. Very kind and always encouraging. Mr. Hokanson could be a bit gruff, but he was a sweetheart, too. I saw him take bags of burgers and drinks out to a family in a station wagon down on their luck. I never forgot that lesson of compassion. They were wonderful people.

CHICKEN DELIGHT:
PRE-COLONEL SANDERS FAIRFIELD FOWL

Taglines and jingles can indelibly imprint a product or restaurant into the minds of customers, and surely, one of the most memorable locally was the one used by Chicken Delight: "Don't cook tonight, call Chicken Delight."

NOW OPEN 'TIL 11 P.M. - DON'T COOK TONIGHT CALL

CHICKEN DELIGHT

DELICIOUS, TASTY AND HOT-TO-YOUR-DOOR.... OVENS IN OUR CARS

• CHICKEN • SHRIMP • B-B-Q RIBS • PIZZA • FISH

Free Delivery*-Ph. 425-9534

OR JUST CALL AND YOUR ORDER MAY BE PICKED UP WITHOUT DELAY

*Within 3 Mile Radius

Chicken Delight Serves Only Fresh Home-Grown Chicken - No "Black Bones" -- No Frozen Chicken Here

Also, we do not pre-cook our chicken, this done to maintain the highest quality as required by Chicken Delight standards. JUST PHONE YOUR ORDER IN AD-VANCE - IT WILL BE READY ON ARRIVAL.

CHICKEN DELIGHT serves plump and meaty, tender grown chicken in the exclusive CHICKEN DELIGHT method. Buckets and sealed serving plates are especially designed so that each dinner may be served individually or for the entire family. No dishes to wash, no food to transfer, just open and eat. AND REMEMBER, it's delivered piping hot to your door, ready to serve.

New, Delicious Menu Items From CHICKEN DELIGHT...

Potato, Macaroni Or Coleslaw Salad
½ Pint 30c

3-Bean Salad ½ Pt 35c

★BLUEBERRY MUFFINS

110 E. TABOR
Just Off No. Travis St.

Complete Dinners or Buckets
Let Us Cater Your Party or Picnic.
Serve 4 to 400 — Hot to Your Door
With Advance Notice — Ph. 425-9534

CHICKEN DELIGHT

DESERT DELIGHT
CHERRY COBBLER
OR APPLE CRISP
35c

★CRISP FRENCH FRIES

FREE DELIVERY
Ph. 425-9534

A 1968 Chicken Delight advertisement. *Fairfield Civic Center Library microfilm.*

The grand opening for Chicken Delight was held on May 19, 1964. It was located at 110 East Tabor Avenue right next to the A&W Drive-In. The business plan was to deliver—within a three-and-half-mile radius from the restaurant—piping-hot chicken dinners. According to a grand-opening

Chicken Delight
110 East Tabor Avenue   425-9534   277

"Don't cook tonight, call Chicken Delight!" They delivered chicken, ribs, shrimp and pizza. *Armijo High yearbook, 1971.*

newspaper advertisement, the complete meal included "half a tender-grown chicken cooked to a rich golden-brown goodness and served with a generous portion of crisp waffle-cut French fries, an old-fashioned blueberry muffin and a delicious serving of tangy cranberry sauce."

There were other delights available as well, including Rib Delight (barbecue loin ribs, French fries, hot sauce, muffin), Shrimp Delight (jumbo shrimp, French fries, shrimp sauce, muffin) and Fish Delight (fish, French fries, tartar sauce, muffin).

Whatever delight a customer settled on, the price was the same: $1.39. In November 1964, it added Pizza Delight, offering freshly baked cheese, sausage, pepperoni or combination pizzas in various sizes. Later, it added other items, like potatoes, macaroni or coleslaw or three-bean salad and Dessert Delight (cherry cobbler or apple crisp).

Chicken Delight started in 1952 in Illinois when an entrepreneur named Al Tunick experimented with cooking different foods in a deep fryer he'd purchased from a restaurant that was going out of business.

At that time, restaurant chicken had mainly been pan-fried, steamed or oven roasted—all of which take some time to cook and precluded it from being a fast-food dish. Tunick coated some chicken in a spicy breading and lowered it into the deep fryer, which cooked it quickly and sealed all the juices inside.

The concept of carry-out and delivery chicken dinners exploded, and soon, Chicken Delight, with the help of its memorable tagline, had housewives rejoicing, as it ballooned to more than one thousand restaurants. Not all of Tunick's ideas were brilliant, however. At one time, he experimented with delivering dinners to area farms by parachuting them from light planes. But nailing where they landed was not a guarantee, and the plan was scrapped.

Locals recalled more than just Chicken Delight's tagline:

Dennis Martin: Bill Southward and I drove the delivery cars with the big chicken on the top. We were the delivery team that got your chicken to you on time and hot! I even drove over a couple of lawns, and Bill slalomed through the Suisun railroad crossing with the arms down.

Doug Rodgers: We had a neighbor who was a total jerk when I was a kid on Kansas Street, so we ordered a meal from Chicken Delight and had it sent to his house for him to pay for. The funny thing is, I ran into him while I was working in water treatment. It turns out, he was an alright [sic] guy; he just didn't like kids in his yard, and he and his wife didn't get along so he was a grump. I told him about the Chicken Delight prank, and we both laughed about it!

Lynn Markle Jewell: My dad managed Chicken Delight for about a year. I was not a fan of chicken before those days and even less so now. Anytime someone called in a false order, guess where the leftover chicken went.

Patti Thoming: On our wedding night, we ordered Chicken Delight delivery to the hotel!

JOHANNE'S HOT DOGS

While numerous local restaurants served hot dogs through the years, usually they were treated as the slightly inferior cousin of hamburgers, which always reigned supreme. That was not the case with Johanne's. Its distinctive frankfurters took center stage from day one. Its tagline was "Home of the Hot Dog That's a Meal in Itself."

The actual date of Johanne's Hot Dogs center stage premiere was August 1, 1970. It was located at 1708 West Texas Street across from West Texas Street Park (which became Allan Witt Park in 1973). The original owners were two independent businessmen, Arnold Brophy and Richard Jacob.

Now, customers could absolutely choose to have a plain ol' ketchup-and-mustard hot dog, but Johanne's had tried to elevate its frankfurter game. Its signature menu item was the Special Dog, which was described in a grand-opening newspaper article as a "specially prepared savory jumbo all meat hot dog, served with juicy red tomato wedges, crisp tangy slices of onion, a perfect dab of spicy relish and snappy mustard."

The restaurant also sold potato chips, a wide variety of beverages, ranging from soft drinks to coffee to milkshakes, and desserts like donuts, apple turnovers and fruit pies. After a year in business, it added chili dogs, cheese dogs, sauerkraut dogs and the double dog. A couple of years later, breakfast items appeared, and locals still rave over Johanne's S.O.S. A rather graphic

SMILING TO GREET YOU as you walk into air conditioned comfort are Arnie Brophy (left) and Rick Jacob (right), owners of Johanne's. They are celebrating their first anniversary this Sat. July 24th and invite everyone to stop in and try one of their delicious hot dogs. — DR Photo by Owens.

Johanne's Hot Dogs owners, Arnie Brophy (*left*) and Rick Jacob (*right*), in 1971. *Fairfield Civic Center Library microfilm.*

A 1973 Johanne's Hot Dogs advertisement. *Fairfield Civic Center Library microfilm.*

U.S. Military term, S.O.S. stands for "Sh—t on a Shingle," and the dish is usually chipped beef stirred into cream sauce and served over toast, but Johanne's used sausage in its dish.

By its second anniversary in 1972, Johanne's ran a promotion in which, for each hot dog they purchased, customers could fill out a form to be entered into a drawing for a pair of tickets to each Oakland Raiders home game. But the East Bay NFL team wasn't the only athletic group Johanne's supported. Little League participants playing across the street at West Texas Street/Allan Witt Park could receive a free hot dog if they hit a home run. The restaurant also did a similar campaign for members of the Fairfield swim team, the Seahorses, who won competitions at the pool there called the Fairfield Plunge.

KENTUCKY FRIED CHICKEN

Although the Fairfield Kentucky Fried Chicken (KFC) is still technically there, it is now in a different location. When it merged with Long John Silver's and opened a drive thru, it moved a grand total of 450 feet.

The original spot first opened its doors in November 1968 with founder Colonel Harland Sanders himself cutting the grand-opening ribbon. One of the innovations Kentucky Fried Chicken introduced was a concept called "sudden service," in which customers did not need to call their order in ahead of time. This was probably just the restaurant's branding way of saying "we will cook a bunch of chicken and put it under heat lamps instead of waiting to cook it when you order it."

The old KFC building was not made with a drive-thru in mind, and converting it to include one proved difficult, as the only place in which to put a drive-thru window was on the opposite side of the building. They tried to MacGyver a solution, and at one point, there was an overhead contraption that was added to facilitate the car-to-restaurant exchange. They finally added a circuitous route to get to the drive-thru before scrapping that idea and moving the whole restaurant.

While most folks visited the restaurant to get a bucket of finger-lickin' good fried chicken seasoned with Colonel Sanders's special recipe of eleven herbs and spices, some evidently came to jam. In a 1968 advertisement, the restaurant announced a giveaway of a twenty-two-minute record album (value three-dollar mono, four-dollar stereo) called *Tijuana Picnic*. The cover featured a family of four having a picnic by a lake and the colonel in the foreground kickin' it against a tree with his own bucket full o' fowl.

The full instrumental album is available on YouTube (http://bit.ly/TijuanaKFC) and features songs like "A Taste of Honey" and "Spanish Flea" in the swingin', toe-tappin' style popularized by Herb Alpert and the Tijuana Brass.

While cockfighting is illegal nearly everywhere, the local old-school chicken fight between KFC, Chicken Delight and Church's Chicken ended years ago with the Colonel being the last crispy bird peddler standing.

HAMBURGERS, INC.

This burger place's rather clunky name matched the odd-shaped building it was housed in at 3001 Travis Boulevard near the Geri-Towne Mall (in 2022 it is Woodcreek Plaza). But at its grand opening in October 1972, it threw down the gauntlet at the burger giant across town with the golden arches that kept a running tally of how many hamburgers it sold. At the bottom of its inaugural advertisement, it boldly said: "Over 11 billion will be sold!"

As it turned out, it didn't sell quite that many, as it was one of the burger spots that not many people remember, but you just had to admire their chutzpah.

YOU'S BURGERS

Hak Soon Yoo along with his wife, Yung Soon Yoo, and their four children emigrated from South Korea in 1973 to the United States. In 1979, they opened You's Burgers at 1615 West Texas Street (later on Second Street) and owned and operated it until 1994.

A 1980 advertisement for the restaurant asked rhetorically, "Where can you go to get a complete meal, including dessert, for only $2.22?" That would include a hamburger with everything on it, French fries, a drink and an ice cream cone. It also offered chili burgers, steak sandwiches, pork sandwiches, grilled cheese, hot dogs, burritos, fish and chips and calamari, among other items.

Locals recalled its tacos and it being the only place in town where you could get a bag full of crinkle-cut fries for a dollar. The youngest Yoo child, Don, grew up to be a captain in the Fairfield Fire Department.

Captain Don Yoo: My parents worked sixteen-plus-hour days almost every day. Christmas and Thanksgiving were their only days off. You's Burgers never made us rich, but we had everything we needed because of it.

BEAMER'S HAMBURGERS

Following in the tradition of Hi-Fi's cheap hamburgers, Beamer's, which opened in 1983, at one point offered a Family Special consisting of a dozen charbroiled hamburgers and six orders of French fries for $5.99. It was located at 1430 North Texas Street, the former Foster's Old Fashion Freeze spot.

Patty O'Brien: They weren't fancy, but they were just plain good.

Johney Pool: Ahhhh, Beamers. Their burgers were so small that we would call them Beamer Biscuits!

3

Classy, Unique, Feedbag

The Spectrum of Fairfield Sit-Down Restaurants

In the United States, there is a restaurant called the Outback Steakhouse, and I could survive in there for several weeks at least, sustaining myself on bloomin' onions and, I'm sure, their legitimate and very Australian cuisine. In the real Outback? I give myself about fourteen minutes.
—Actor Steve Carell

Casual dining (or sit-down) restaurants typically serve moderately priced food in a relaxed atmosphere. The following were establishments that ran the gamut from your uber-fancy-schmancy dining experiences to those that were basically about customers being able to shovel as much cuisine into their gullets as they could before the owners made them leave.

If you don't see a particular restaurant here, it might mean that it is mentioned elsewhere in this book. Or it could just mean that it is one of the myriad that I simply could not give space to. Don't take it personally. These are also not presented in any particular order or ranking.

DICK'S RESTAURANT: WHAT'S IN A NAME?

Originally, this section about the restaurant owned by Dick and Dee Stellina was going to be a part of chapter 6, "Reincarnated Restaurants." That's

Dick's Restaurant

1620 Pennsylvania   425-5285

Dick's Restaurant's decor sported a tropical theme that was echoed by the menu. *Armijo High yearbook, 1970.*

because after it was Dick's, it became BJ's, the Fairfield Express and Tony Roma's: A Place for Ribs. But Dick's seemed to be in a constant state of reincarnation itself. Take the name: the official name changed several times, and there are newspaper advertisements, yearbook advertisements, matchbook covers and more, all with similar but different names. They include Dick's, Dick's Restaurant, Dick's Steaks, Dick's Wonderful Food, Dick's Tropical Restaurant and Dick's Seafood Grotto.

Whatever you call it, the Stellina's restaurant was located at 1620 Pennsylvania Avenue, opened in the 1950s and was not a casual dining spot. Fairfielders dressed up when they went to Dick's place and expected wonderful service and world-class food.

The menu and theme of the restaurant was an evolving affair as well. At one point in the late 1950s, Dick's offered not just American dishes, like steaks, but Chinese (specifically Cantonese) fare as well. In 1960, the tropical theme was adopted with South Sea Island dinners and exotic rum drinks as their specialty.

Dick Stellina evidently was a big believer in advertising, as many examples are easily found in the historical record. He was constantly trying to elevate and heighten awareness of his local brand.

In the spring of 1968, Fairfield's Architectural Approval Committee declined approval of a new sign for his establishment. While the committee had approved a use permit, allowing for an increase in the sign area that Stellina wished to use, it had other issues with his proposal. The committee reviewed the requested signage and declared it to be "tawdry and unrefined, particularly in relationship to the existing development which was sophisticated and restful."

What happened next at the meeting may not have been a dramatic "Perry Mason" moment, but the reporter who wrote the newspaper piece about it sure made it seem like one:

> *To show how wonderful his sign was, Mr. Stellina ordered the house lights dimmed. He then proceeded to plug in the sign, which he had brought with him to the meeting and all of its thirty-six lights glowed eerily in the council chambers. For what seemed like an eternity, all present stared at the glowing lights, and when the spell was broken and the lights of the chambers again were turned on, all on the commission expressed their satisfaction that the sign was not as had been described by the Architectural Approval Committee.*

The sign was approved with two conditions: that the existing roof signs on the building be removed and that the proposed sign be "non-flashing and non-scintillating."

Locals shared dressed-up memories of Dick's Restaurant:

> *Mitchell Walker: It was one of the best restaurants in Fairfield at the time. It had a room in the back with a putting green. My folks met there in the mid '50s.*

> *Sharon Kneezle Soliere: Dick's is where I went to my first prom dinner. I went with Steve Reed from the Armijo class of 1965, who ended up marrying my sister Gail!*

> *Fairfield Mayor Gary Falati: The Fairfield City Council is much more political today than back when I was on it. Not necessarily partisan, but political. We used to do the people's business and then all go to Dick's Seafood Grotto together afterward.*

> *Bill Roberts: Good food. I remember the bamboo and fish nets.*

> *Susan Macy Luckenbach: They had peacock chairs, and it was supposed to be kind of a Hawaiian theme, so they had palm fronds that came from the*

trees that lined the street leading up to my cousins the Lambrechts house in Suisun Valley (now called the Blue Victorian). The fire department found out they had dried palm fronds, and they had to take them out.

They had a round copper fireplace in the bar area and my stepdad and my mother loved to go there. I was an only child at the time. Dick's had a Hawaiian band, and as you walked in, there was a waterfall and a fishpond. One time, my stepdad rolled his pants legs up put on a grass skirt and started doing the hula. I wanted to crawl under the table.

We would have dinner there every Friday night. Dick and Dee were friends of the family. I was pretty little, so I usually went in my pajamas and a bathrobe. After dinner, my stepdad would put me in the back seat of the car to sleep while my parents partied. Can you imagine doing that now?

BEHOLD! VOICI

From what I have been able to ascertain, the French word *voici* (pronounced "vwa-see") roughly translates to "behold" in English. When many locals behold the rundown husk of the former Voici restaurant at 1721 North Texas Street, they may have a very hard time believing that at one time it was the swankiest spot in town.

Voici had its grand opening on September 14, 1960. Floor-to-ceiling windows overlooked a small, well-kept garden. The interior featured white tablecloths, turquoise upholstered chairs and blooming African violets at each table. Gold-framed paintings, pictures, antique mirrors and decorative cake plates graced the walls. The waitresses wore pastel gingham pinafore uniforms. It was one of the few Fairfield restaurants that people remember where men were expected to wear a jacket and tie when dining.

Voici was known for its steaks, lobster tails and chicken sauté. It used fresh, in-season vegetables, and its salad dressing was made from scratch using fresh country eggs. A popular menu item was its hot garlic or cheese French bread. Complete dinners included soup, salad, an entrée, vegetables, bread, dessert and a beverage and started at $3.95 (about $27.00 in 2022).

Soon, regular guests came from as far away as Stockton and Sacramento, and it was the go-to spot for Fairfielders' prom dates and anniversaries.

The owners, Juanita Musso and her husband, William, had owned Vallejo restaurants the Bank Club, the Rex Café and the Brass Rail tavern before moving east to Fairfield.

Above: An advertisement celebrating Voici's tenth anniversary in 1970. *Fairfield Civic Center Library microfilm.*

Left: A Voici advertisement that ran after the original owner, Juanita Musso's, death. *Fairfield Civic Center Library microfilm.*

At Christmastime, Musso decorated the inside of Voici with ornaments hanging from the ceiling, including some that were three feet long. She crafted all of them by hand, and since she added to her collection each year, over time, they took over a whole room in her house.

Voici was also a local spot for Solano County movers and shakers to meet.

Fairfield Mayor Gary Falati: We had a Solano County Mayor's Conference, and it was now-supervisor and then–newly elected Suisun City mayor Jim Spering's first one. Afterward, we all went to Voici for a drink. We needed to appoint one of us to the MTC. [The Metropolitan Transportation Commission (MTC) is the transportation planning, financing and coordinating agency for the nine-county San Francisco Bay Area.] *Spering, as the new kid on the block, drew the shortest straw.*

Suisun City Mayor/Solano County Supervisor Jim Spering: I think they were sticking me with it. I didn't even know what the hell it was, but I sure learned quickly. That was in December 1986. I'm now [in 2022] *the longest-serving commissioner, and I've worked with wonderful staff and lots of legislators, and we've been able to do some great things for Solano County. And it all started at Voici.*

While it was not burglarized with anywhere near the regularity of the old Octo Inn decades before, one successful break-in at Voici netted more than all of the break-ins at the former eight-sided eatery combined. On October 30, 1967, thieves got away with more than $17,000 (more than $140,000 in 2022) after they cut a three-inch hole in the office safe. Musso said that some of the money and jewels that were taken had been given to her to keep by friends.

Police photographs showed a professional-looking torch-cut three-inch hole in the restaurant's office safe. According to Musso, the safe had $4,400 in cash, two women's platinum rings valued together at $8,750 and a diamond pendant worth $4,000. It was one of the largest heists in Fairfield's history.

The article made no mention of why a restaurant kept such valuable property on its premises.

After owning Voici for the better part of two decades, Juanita Musso died in July 1980. In 1981, a new ownership team consisting of Glenn Karnet, Chuck and Vera Hartke and Geno Salvitti took over.

That year, a reporter from the Sacramento Bee stopped by Voici and wrote a favorable review:

In a culinary wasteland of practically every fast-food franchise you can name, Voici stands out like an oasis in the Sahara. It's pleasantly appointed, with candles and white linen on the tables, cloth napkins, good crystal and flatware and outdoor greenery to screen off the flow of traffic, which otherwise would be seen through the picture window. Voici makes no pretensions at being a garden of exotic epicurean delights; what it is is a first-class example of a basic American dinner house, the only concession to ethnicity being veal scaloppini and Bordelaise sauce—both of which were tried to our satisfaction.

Despite the review, the dining-out times, they were a-changin' in Fairfield. The convenience and price points of fast food were beginning to trump elegant dining for many locals, and Voici's bottom line took several uppercuts and gut punches.

Also, a number of decisions were made by the new owners that hastened the restaurant's demise. In July 1983, they held a Christmas in July event and sold off all the beautiful handmade ornaments that, for years, had been a Voici Yuletide staple. Then its grand reopening included a much larger change: the name of the restaurant became Diana's, named after Geno Salvitti's sister.

Eventually, the once-fancy eatery was sold, and its grandeur faded into obscurity.

Locals shared exquisite memories of Voici:

> *Janette Lobdell: My best friend Joan Hopkins's parents took me there once. I remember telling my mom, that they came around and put salad dressing on my salad out of a fancy little pitcher. My mom teased me, asking if they cut my meat for me.*

> *Christy Thompson: I only went once when I was a young teenager, and it was a very big deal. I had the shrimp salad and can still taste it in my mind.*

> *Erica M. Kimes: I was having dinner with my family when all the adults got up and went into the bar to see Nixon resign on TV.*

> *Debbie Nunez: My prom date took me there for dinner before the dance. I married him!*

> *Susan Macy Luckenback: I went there once. It was a higher-end restaurant. I never actually ate there because my then-husband, Ed Luckenback, worked for the city of Fairfield, and he had a big red beard and mustache and hair that was not that long but longer than normal, and they wouldn't serve us. They said "Sorry, we're full." I looked around, and there were like two people in there.*

> *Roy Word III: We were an NCO military family, so to dine at such a place was literally beyond my dad's pay grade. The saving up to eat at such a place took a while. The dress code was a coat and tie.*

> *Peggy Cato: I had my first fancy dinner with my date there. We have been married for over forty-five years, so I guess it was a fantastic dinner!*

Voici Chicken Sauté
By Original Chef Cecil Villanueva

1 three-pound chicken, cut into eight pieces
¼ cup flour
2 tablespoons butter or margarine
salt and pepper
2 cups sliced fresh mushrooms
1 cup au jus (from mix)
1 tablespoon chicken base
¼ cup each sherry and sauterne wine
1 tablespoon chopped green onion
1 tablespoon chopped celery

Instructions: Dust chicken pieces with flour; brown in hot oil and butter. Season with salt and pepper. Place browned chicken in nine-by-thirteen-inch baking pan. Sprinkle on mushrooms. Prepare au jus according to directions on package; stir in chicken base, sherry and sauterne wine, mixing well. Pour over chicken and mushrooms in pan. Bake, uncovered, in 350-degree preheated oven for about forty-five minutes or until desired doneness, basting occasionally. When done, arrange on hot serving platter; sprinkle on onion and parsley. Makes two very generous servings.

THE FIREHOUSE DELI CAFÉ

On November 19, 1949, a local radio program called *Fairfield-Suisun on the Air* broadcast and recorded the opening ceremony for a new Fairfield Firehouse, located at 620 Jackson Street. It was Fairfield's first city-owned building. Several dignitaries were called on to speak and celebrate the $31,000 project (over $362,000 in 2022) that had been funded by a bond measure. They included California Assemblyman Ernest Crowley, Fairfield Mayor Clyde Jean, Fire Commissioner and City Councilman Allan Witt, Councilman Joseph Gerevas, Fire Chief/Police Chief Rex Clift and others.

The exterior of the Firehouse Deli-Café that faced Jackson Street. *Courtesy of Victor DeStefani.*

While a sizable contingent showed up for the celebration, the expected numbers were a tad smaller than predicted, as some were siphoned off by the Armijo football game as well as a Cal-Stanford game.

At the ceremony, refreshments were served that included sandwiches, coffee and soft drinks. It was the first time sandwiches were offered at that location, but it would not be the last.

The firehouse was in use for nearly twenty years until it became a teen center in 1968.

Enter Victor DeStefani.

DeStefani was the co-owner and manager of the supermarket inside the iconic department store Wonder World from its opening in 1964 until 1978. "In 1970, Fairfield city manager B. Gale Wilson stopped by Wonder World and suggested that I buy the firehouse. It was a teen club, and they were beating the hell out of it, so the city decided to sell it," DeStefani said in a 2019 interview. "I talked to my wife, and at that time, it was becoming the thing for restaurants to be located in old banks and other buildings. We got it and the adjoining parking lot for the asking price of $25,000, since there were no other bids."

Victor DeStefani's wife, LaReece, had a flair for antiques and interior decorating, and the deli/restaurant featured authentic trappings of turn-of-the-century firefighting. The Suisun Fire Protection District restored two custom-made firehose carts that LaReece bought in Utah, and local departments would borrow them for the hose cart races at Suisun City musters. They also added a brass fireman's pole that Victor DeStefani described as "gorgeous."

The Firehouse Deli Café was an immediate hit when it opened in December 1971. "The first day it opened, it was unbelievable, and it never quit. That's because it was one of a kind," DeStefani said.

The café's decor was authentic—and sometimes a bit too authentic. "The old siren was left on top, and at noon, it would go off. We finally had to disconnect it after about three months because it was scaring customers," DeStefani said.

While the novelty of the firehouse attracted customers, what kept them coming back was the food. The Firehouse Deli Café billed itself in advertisements as "Fairfield's Only Real Delicatessen." It backed up that bold assertion by offering meats, cheeses, salads, pastries, beer, wine, sarsaparilla and much more. "We put in a twenty-four-foot-long deli case and made 148 different sandwiches. We had a forty-gallon steam kettle we used to make all of our spaghetti sauce there. The sauce was my mother's recipe. She was

A 1972 Firehouse Deli-Café advertisement touting just a fraction of the foodstuffs they offered. *Fairfield Civic Center Library microfilm.*

from Italy. She used sausage, tomato sauce, onions and lots of garlic—all that good stuff," DeStefani said.

LaReece DeStefani read in a restaurant trade magazine about the advisability of hiring school cooks for their vast experience, so she hired LaVeta Gregerson and Frances Swank, who'd worked for the Fairfield-Suisun Unified School District and both helped to perfect the menu.

The restaurant was a family affair, and the DeStefanis' children, Vicki, Daneece, Robin and Todd, all worked there and contributed to keeping the business afloat.

The amount of menu items the Firehouse Deli Café featured was staggering. Meat and cheese trays, apple and pumpkin mince and many other varieties of pies, smoked oysters, assorted breads—it offered so much, it was obvious it could branch out if desired, so it did.

The DeStefanis opened the Snack Shack located at the Texaco Truck Stop off Interstate 80 and Suisun Valley Road in Cordelia. There, they served breakfast and many of the Firehouse favorite sandwiches and dinners seven days a week.

Back across town at the Firehouse, the upstairs area where the firefighters used to sleep was a separate antique gift shop run by French national Monique Jones and her husband, Ben, called Antique Legend. When it closed after a few years, LaReece DeStefani saw an opportunity. She turned it into a dining area called the Bedroom Steak House. Bed headboards and footboards served as partitions between tables. She also added a unique salad bar—an ice-filled brass bathtub. Thus, the restaurant's tagline, "Enjoy salad in the tub and your favorite steak in bed," was born.

The 1976 Bedroom menu included, among other things: the Noon Siren (a steak sandwich on a French roll with French fries, $3.95), Spontaneous Ignition (cheese lasagna with meat sauce, $3.50) and the Towering Inferno (roast beef sandwich with mushrooms, onion, pepper, cheese, $2.79). Coffee, tea, milk and soft drinks were listed under "extinguishers," and beer and wine were called "resuscitators."

The DeStefanis sold the restaurant in 1978. They then owned and operated a number of grocery stores in the Sacramento area called Vic's IGA Markets. IGA stands for the Independent Grocers Alliance, which is an organization that brings together independent grocers across the United States and in thirty other countries to level the playing field with the larger chain grocery outlets. They worked until they were in their early eighties before finally retiring in 2010.

LaReece DeStefani by the bathtub salad bar in the Firehouse Deli-Café. *Courtesy of Victor DeStefani.*

LaReece DeStefani died in 2015, and Victor followed her in 2021. Locals reflected on the Firehouse Deli Cafe:

Sherri Salcido Leon: The one and only place to get pastrami way back then.

Rhonda Murray: My friend and I would get the best ham and Swiss cheese sandwiches on rye bread with potato salad there once a month. We cut class at high school just for that.

Mark Smith: The noon whistle was actually the horn to summon volunteer firefighters in the event of a fire. Sounding it every day at noon was how they tested it to make sure it worked while at the same time not causing all the volunteers to come running to the station because they knew the test would be at noon. I wonder what would have happened if they had had a real fire at noon and none of the firefighters showed up.

Janet Cline Kohlwes: We took my parents to dinner there and announced we were pregnant with our first child. My mother was thrilled; my father wasn't. He said he was going to stop accepting our invitations to dinner if we kept springing news like that on him.

MUFFIN TREAT

The first Carl's Jr. restaurant opened in Fairfield in 1978, but nearly thirty years before that, a sound-alike eatery opened just a mile and a half down North Texas Street. Karl's Drive-In, a burger joint housed in a forty-by-fifty-two-foot rustic redwood building, first opened for business on July 5, 1950.

The location, at what was then the junction of old and new Highway 40, or 3333 North Texas Street, meant it could entice hungry east–west motorists to stop and try one of the Big Boy Hamburgers on a toasted French bun and other fountain items. It was also an ideal spot to attract customers from right across the street at a business that opened the same month, the Solano Drive-In Theatre.

Karl's Drive-In was short-lived and has faded into obscurity. The restaurant that most Fairfielders associate with that spot is the one owned and operated by Glenn and Ellie Coleman, Muffin Treat. It opened on Mother's Day weekend in 1966 and was an immediate hit. It was so much of a hit that a week later, the owners felt compelled to put an advertisement in the *Daily Republic* apologizing because it had to close early during the grand opening to serve the people already seated and waiting. It read, "We expected *some* of you to come, but not *all*. We have only excuses, excuses, excuses. Please do come and see us again."

In addition to its prime rib au jus and other offerings, Muffin Treat also had a popular cocktail lounge called the Moon Room at the north end of the building that featured local and regional musical artists and dancing. A newspaper advertisement described it as having "plush seating and carpeting, a nice dance floor, a long, comfortable bar and a cozy sunken fireplace alcove."

Carol Bratton was a long-term waitress at Muffin Treat and remembered how pleasant most folks were. That even included a gentleman wearing a nice business suit on the way to a meeting that she spilled a chocolate soda all over. She also remembered another waitress letting an egg slip off a plate and onto the head of a customer. He was bald, so he wound up with more egg than hair.

Above: Muffin Treat was a right-off-the-freeway Fairfield institution for thirty years. *Fairfield High yearbook, 1973.*

Left: The interior of the Muffin Treat. *Armijo High yearbook, 1974.*

The Colemans ran the Muffin Treat for a number of years, and after they passed away, their son Steve and his wife, Cathy, took it over. Steve knew the business, as he had worked in it from the time he was a little kid, having to stand on a box to wash dishes.

The Muffin Treat was sold in 1995, and a new eatery named Lou's Junction opened there. Unfortunately, Lou's was destroyed in a raging fire in 2005. In 2009, Texas Roadhouse opened in the oft-traveled spot.

Fairfielders shared memories of Muffin Treat on Facebook:

Mike Roberts: I worked at Muffin Treat in the '80s. I worked the late shift, so a couple of friends and I closed the kitchen down. Once the Moon Room closed, it was on like Donkey Kong! Can you say, "Open Bar?"

Bobby Morris: In 1972, I applied for a dishwasher job. I got turned down during the interview and was told, "We don't hire your type!" My type was "hair too long." Quite an eye-opener for me!

Anita Schmitt-Ford: Muffin Treat was home to the Moon Room or the "Menopause Lounge," as it was referred to by us youngsters back in the day. Now, I'd be a patron!

Allen Grundvig: Bachman-Turner Overdrive were regulars.

Jeff Johnson: I worked there for three years. It was Lou's Junction, and the bar was the Captain's Lounge. I was in shock watching it burn on the news in the morning before I left for work in Sacramento.

Bruce Gross: It was a huge fire. All those years of grease up in the vents. The firehouse across the street saw it first. It had a fully involved roof by the time they got the engine there.

Joyce Matzen: I met Pat Morita (from Happy Days *and* The Karate Kid*) at the Muffin Treat. He was the nicest man.*

Christine Todd: The Moon Room was where men could NOT wear tank tops, but girls could wear anything they wanted.

LYON'S

A Lyon's advertisement from 1983. *Fairfield Civic Center Library microfilm.*

I don't think it's a stretch to refer to the old Lyon's restaurant, which was located at 2390 North Texas Street next door to Carl's Jr., as a slightly more upscale version of Denny's. Soon after it opened in 1977, local service organizations began holding their monthly meetings, as well as special events, in the restaurant's large banquet hall.

The location, right next to Air Base Parkway, was convenient for a spot that was open twenty-four hours a day. Lyon's served American breakfasts with hearty portions, and repeat customers came for the decades it occupied that spot.

Lyon's was founded in San Francisco in the early 1950s. Its relatively high-end coffee shop appeal was popular, and it served bacon, eggs and waffles but also included French dip sandwiches, liver and onions, teriyaki mushroom burgers, beef kabobs and prime rib dinners on its menu, and it had a full bar as well.

Consolidated Foods Corporation, which later became Sara Lee, bought the Lyon's chain in 1966. It changed hands, went through bankruptcy proceedings and all the things struggling restaurants do until its final death rattle. The Fairfield location later became Jack and Linda's County Café and then the Benicia Grill II.

Lyon's memories, as shared from locals:

Michelle Klein: My grandparents owned the corner lot they built the restaurant on. It used to have the Klein Motel, my grandfather's mobile home sales and my grandmother's furniture store there.

Fairfield Mayor Gary Falati: At a city council meeting, I once bet a political opponent $100 that we could bring a Costco here and got criticized for betting in the council chambers. Then the sheriff Al Cardoza saw me at Lyon's Restaurant, put me in cuffs and said he had to arrest me for gambling!

81

Janine Lomina: I think I spent my entire senior year there discussing philosophy and life over a million cups of coffee.

Mona Garcia: I worked at the Fairfield Lyon's, and I remember waiting on Freddie Stubbs, who played Rerun on the TV show What's Happening! *He asked me to join him on his boat that he had docked in Suisun after I got off of work, but I politely declined.*

Kevin Tenney: I hung out there so much, I ended up dating a couple of the waitresses.

Glenn Stubbs: I had four twenty-first birthdays in the Lyons bar…starting when I was seventeen!

Celina Mae: Sometimes, there are Facebook posts of advertisements from old restaurants that, in your mind, you can almost smell. A Lyon's one I saw smelled like clam chowder, garlic bread…and cigarettes.

THE OLD SAN FRANCISCO EXPRESS

Similar to how the Firehouse Deli Café repurposed an old building into a memorable restaurant, the Old San Francisco Express used out-of-service train cars to create a unique family casual dining spot that was adjacent to a gift shop.

It started out as the Cordelia Junction Restaurant and had its grand opening on July 26, 1978. The menu featured prime rib, steak and seafood and had a sixteen-foot-long salad bar. Doug Saladino and Steve Preston transformed the Cordelia Junction Restaurant into the Old San Francisco Express in the early 1980s.

Green Valley resident Chris Veenbaas worked as a chef there for eight years and shared some remembrances. "We'd do between five hundred to seven hundred dinners on the weekends. Back then, everything was made from scratch. Our specialty was prime rib and of course the minestrone soup. The cold storage train car is where we kept all the meat, produce and dairy. A lot of beer was drank [sic] back there playing quarters from 1981 to 1989."

The restaurant was popular with Interstate 80 motorists intrigued by the unique theme, Green Valley residents who enjoyed a nice sit-down meal and other Fairfielders who made the brief trip for their favorite dishes.

16 ft. long

New Salad Bar
Now Open!

Offering:

Minestrone soup and soup of the day - 24 cool, fresh salad toppings on each side. A variety of fresh vegetables, nuts and 8 assorted salads per side. Also baked potatoes and several delicious choices for toppings.

Doug Saladino, owner of Old San Francisco Express, and Chef Christopher Veenbaas recently announced the opening of the new salad bar as well as new lunch and dinner menus. All innovations are apart of the recent remodeling at Old San Francisco Express.

New lunch and dinner menus are in effect.

| Champagne Brunch Sunday 10 a.m.-2 p.m. Lunch M-Sat. 11 a.m.-4 p.m. | | Dinner M-Th 4 p.m.-10 p.m. F-Sat. 4 p.m.-11 p.m. Sunday 2 p.m.-10 p.m. |

I-80 & 680 at Cordelia Junction ● Call 864-1900

A 1988 advertisement for the Old San Francisco Express. *Fairfield Civic Center Library microfilm.*

The brisk business the eatery was doing did not go unnoticed by those with less than honorable intentions. In December 1981, some thieving Scrooge broke in through a window and used a cutting torch and pry tools to relieve the restaurant's safe of over $17,000. Actually, the crook was more like the Grinch than Scrooge, as he even stopped to pry open a cigarette machine for change with the $17,000 in hand and stole three bottles of beer, a briefcase and some art supplies. There was no word on if he took their Christmas tree, decorations and Who Hash as well.

Since it was right off the freeway, many celebrities would stop by the Old San Francisco Express on their way to Tahoe. They included Jerry Mathers, who played the titular role on the '50s TV show *Leave It to Beaver*, singer/songwriter Barry Manilow and country music duet the Judds, among others.

The restaurant closed in 2001, but the Cordelia Antique Mall is still plugging away in 2022. They even sometimes field phone calls from people hoping to make dinner reservations at the now-long-gone restaurant.

The one menu item that many locals remark about, even to this day, is the minestrone soup. Veenbaas used to make it in two sixty-gallon kettles but through trial and error adapted it to the home version that is made as follows:

The Old San Francisco Express Minestrone Soup Recipe
Chris Veenbaas

I pound red beans
6–8 ounces diced or ground salt pork
½ cup crushed fresh garlic
I small yellow onion, diced
I teaspoon crushed dry red pepper
I tablespoon ground Italian herbs
4 carrots, chopped
½ head of cabbage
3 quarts seasoned beef stock
I eight-ounce can of tomato paste,
8 ounces small-shell pasta

Instructions: Soak beans covered in water overnight and then drain. Cook beans until soft and then mash them. In a tall-sided skillet, toss in your diced/ground salt pork and, when browned, toss in your garlic, onions and crushed red pepper. Let it all sweat down until the garlic is cooked. Toss in your Italian herbs, stir, then set to the side.

Using a stock pot, add your veggies with a quart of seasoned-to-taste beef stock. When the veggies come to a boil, turn the heat down, add your crushed cooked beans and your soup base. Stir well, then add your tomato paste and turn the heat back up. Let it simmer for a while, then add your pasta. Stir every three minutes with heat on medium for ten minutes. If too thick, add water, season to taste and enjoy!

HOWARD JOHNSON'S: HOJOS ON THE HILL

Back in the day, if passing motorists could spot a roadside restaurant with an orange roof, they didn't even need to see the sign to know it was a Howard Johnson's.

In the 1920s, Howard Deering Johnson bought a small soda shop in Quincy, Massachusetts, and customers soon marveled at his homemade ice cream, which doubled the butterfat of competitors. Eventually, it became known for having twenty-eight flavors decades before Baskin-Robbins did them three flavors better. The first Howard Johnson's restaurant opened in Quincy in the late 1920s, and its menu featured hot dogs, baked beans, ice cream and fried clams.

Franchises exploded in the 1930s, and they became ubiquitous. The aqua interiors can be credited (or blamed) on socialite Sister Parish, whom Howard Johnson hired. She later decorated the White House for the Kennedy administration.

Fairfield's Howard Johnson's opened in late 1972 and had its grand opening on January 11, 1973. It was located at the top of the hill near the Interstate 80 North Texas onramp. Its grand-opening specials included steak and clams or steak and shrimp.

Patrons recall the Fudgana, which was a banana split–esque creation that had hot fudge and whipped cream, the Moo Cow plastic creamer dispensers and the Double Bubble cocktails, which were two drinks for one price.

The all-you-can-eat menu included ribs, chicken, roast beef and roast turkey, but the tender, sweet fried clams are what take up the most real estate in the memories of many Fairfielders.

Competition from other diners and the fast-food boom coupled with menus rooted in the same fare that had been popular in the '60s and '70s

The Fairfield Howard Johnson's sign and exterior in 1991. *Courtesy of Phil Edwards, www. highwayhos.org.*

Left: Howard Johnson's grand opening advertisement from 1973. *Fairfield Civic Center Library microfilm.*

Right: A 1981 advertisement for a Howard Johnson's pajama party. *Fairfield Civic Center Library microfilm.*

doomed Howard Johnson's in the '80s. The Fairfield location held on valiantly before closing in the early 1990s.

Locals shared memories of HoJo's:

> *James Fife: I drove there on my motorcycle at night in the rain to get onion rings because of my wife's pregnancy cravings.*

> *Gloria Jean Lee: Loved it! In the '60s, we met two wrestlers there, Ray Stevens and Pepper Gomez.*

> *Kimberly Snyder: I remember going there as a kid and the wait staff asking my parents if they wanted to sit in the smoking or nonsmoking section. Even though we always sat in nonsmoking, I still smelled smoke.*

RED TOP DAIRY/RESTAURANT

The Red Top Dairy, headquartered in Vallejo, was owned by Albert Ferrari from 1940 to 1981. It was a meager operation at first in a building on Marin and Main Streets, but by 1944, the company moved to a larger spot on Broadway Street. Soon, a distribution center run by Floyd "Red" Widger was started in Fairfield at 505 Jefferson Street (in 2022, it is a closed bail bonds business). Widger had a very short work commute, as he and his wife, Mary, lived next door on the corner of Jefferson and Delaware Streets.

Many old-timers fondly recall having fresh Red Top milk delivered to their homes in wire racks that held their trademark brown glass bottles.

Not to be confused with Red Top Fountain discussed in chapter 1, for many Fairfield longtimers, the memory that is conjured by the term "Red Top" is the restaurant and dairy that opened in 1963 and used to be located at 8001 Lincoln Highway (now Interstate 80). Like Howard Johnson's down the freeway, Red Top could be identified just by the color of its roof—obviously crimson.

The little Vallejo dairy that could soon became a regional behemoth—a huge, ultramodern bottling plant that served customers all over Solano County and beyond. The operation was so successful that the very street address where the dairy/restaurant was located was changed to 199 Red Top Road.

The literally right-off-the-freeway location couldn't be missed, and the restaurant's visibility was aided by its bright-red roof. During Christmastime, it featured an elaborate Nativity scene complete with actual livestock.

Fairfield High School class of 1977 graduate Becky Brooks Yarrow was a waitress at Red Top from 1976 to 1981 and remembered flirting with CHP officers, getting tips from happy gamblers coming back from Reno and having fun with her brother Mike, who also worked there. She once had a close encounter with a major celebrity at the restaurant and almost missed it. "I waited on Al Pacino, and I still have the coffee cup he signed for me. When he was sitting at the counter, I didn't realize who he was, but another waitress told me, so I chased after him when he was leaving," Yarrow said.

The twenty-four-hour Red Top Restaurant was a favorite spot for locals and freeway passersby to get their fix of to-die-for hot fudge sundaes, banana splits, milkshakes, spaghetti and much more. That all ended Saturday, June 20, 1981.

On that fateful day, a welder severed a high-pressure hydraulic line, sparking a fire. It soon became an inferno, with flames leaping thirty feet in the air. Firefighters from Cordelia, Suisun City, Fairfield, Vallejo, Mare Island

A clipping from a 1981 article about the fire at Red Top. *Fairfield Civic Center Library microfilm.*

and American Canyon battled the blaze and were successful in keeping it away from toxic chemical storage tanks in the dairy processing plant. Seven people were hurt, and the restaurant burned to the ground. The damage was estimated to cost about $8 million (more than $23 million in 2021).

There is never a good time for a lucrative landmark business to be lost, but the timing of Red Top Restaurant's fiery demise was especially brutal. It had just been bought by a joint venture formed between Raley's, Bel Air and Save Mart grocery stores and had been in operation for less than three weeks when the blaze claimed it.

The dairy was rebuilt and reopened in 1983, but the new roof was blue, and there was no restaurant. It was never the same.

Locals left with just memories of Red Top milkshakes and more shared their thoughts about the eatery:

> *Dan Monez: When I worked for the Solano Sheriff's Office (1973–84), the only places open for graveyard-shift deputies to eat or grab a cup of coffee were the Red Top, the Cordelia Truck Stop and the Brigadoon Restaurant in Vacaville. Red Top was my favorite!*

> *Tricia Bracy: I remember the cow syrup dispensers. I miss that place. Damn welders!*

> *Denise Spielman: I used to work there. I had just gotten home from my shift the day it burned down. I drove right back, and it was unbelievable.*

> *Linda Wilson: My husband was a bus boy there…until he ate the ears off of an ice cream bunny.*

> *Billy Gear: All the chocolate milk you could drink for a quarter = gastric regret.*

HOLIDAY INN

It probably goes without saying that *American Idiot*, *Spamalot* and *Urinetown*, three popular modern musicals, would make horrible names for a hotel chain. And yet, the name for one of America's most popular and successful hotels, Holiday Inn, came from the 1942 Bing Crosby musical film of the same name.

Holiday Inn was founded by Charles Kemmons Wilson, and the first one opened in Memphis, Tennessee, in 1952. They began popping up all over the country and soon lived up to the company's tagline: "Your host from coast to coast."

The Fairfield Holiday Inn opened in 1971, and an advertisement touted the iconic "great sign" it was known for. The sign, which featured 1,500 feet of neon tubing and more than five hundred incandescent light bulbs, was described as "a lavish mark on the Solano County Skyline." Never mind that Solano County didn't and doesn't actually have a skyline—it still sounded pretty darn good.

Incidentally, the "great sign" was Holiday Inn's most successful form of advertising, and Charles Kemmons Wilson loved it so much that a replica is engraved on his tombstone with the word "Founder" in the marquee and the arrow pointing to his name.

In addition to over 140 rooms (with color TVs) and a lounge, the Fairfield Holiday Inn featured its own restaurant as well. Lifelong Fairfielder Toni Todd worked there for about ten years as the head supervisor.

> *I worked there when* [Fairfield developer and philanthropist] *Billy Gene Yarbrough had it. He was so sweet and caring, and he only wanted me to serve him. One particular incident I remember there was when I had helped a customer and was going to run his credit card, and it had the last name Gates on it. It was the early '90s and around the time of the Rodney King incident, and LA police chief Daryl Gates was in the news. So, I thought it was him, but it wasn't. It was Bill Gates and his then fiancée. Kris Kristofferson also stayed there, and I just missed getting an autograph because as I ran out of the restaurant, he was pulling away in a black limousine.*

Eventually, the Holiday Inn was sold, and as of 2022, the Courtyard Marriott occupies its old space.

ANNOUNCING OUR NEW MENU AT THE
APACHE DINING ROOM & COFFEE SHOP

**CHEF
FRANK M. SCHINKA**

SEA FOOD DINNERS

SPECIAL SEA FOOD PLATE	2.45
Sole, Oysters, Prawns, Scallops, Tartar Sauce	
FILET OF SOLE, Meuniere	2.10
LOBSTER THERMIDOR	3.95
LOBSTER SAUTE EN WINE	4.00
BROILED LOBSTER TAIL	3.85
FRENCH FRIED SHRIMP	2.25
With Hot Sauce	
FRENCH FRIED OYSTERS	2.25
with Tarter Sauce	
FRENCH FRIED SCALLOPS	2.25
with Tarter Sauce	
FRIED HALIBUT	1.95
FRIED RAINBOW TROUT (2)	2.20
with Lemon Butter	
CRAB CURRY with Rice	2.25
SHRIMP CURRY with Rice	2.15
BAKED CRAB, au Gratin	2.25
BAKED SHRIMP, au Gratin	2.15
FRENCH FRIED FROG LEGS	3.00

SPECIAL N.Y. STEAK 1.95
Bite Size
French Fries and Salad
French Bread

BAR-B-Q SANDWICHES ____ 85c
Beef, Ham or Turkey with French Fries

HOT SANDWICHES

New York Steak Sandwich	1.95
Hot Beef Sandwich, Potatoes	1.10
Hot Turkey Sandwich, Potatoes	1.10
Beef Dip on French Bread, French Fries	1.10
Special Denver Sandwich	85c
Hot Dog on Roll	40c

SANDWICHES

Chiliburger	85c	Deviled Egg	50c
Hamburger	50c	Grilled Cheese	55c
Cheeseburger	65c	Boiled Ham	65c
Chicken Salad	60c	Roast Turkey	85c
Tuna Fish	55c	Cold Beef	70c
DeLuxe Hamburger			65c
Corned Beef on Rye			75c
Grilled Ham and Cheese			85c
Bacon and Tomato			60c
Lettuce and Tomato			45c
Club House Sandwich			1.35

CHILI

Chili Bowl	50c
Chili Dog	60c
Ground Chili Steak	1.45

May We Suggest One Of
Cadenasso's Fine Wines
For Your Dining Pleasure
HOUSE SPECIALS
Burgundy .... Chablis
Pinot Noir .... Vin Rose
Sauterne
Fifth $1.50

CHILDREN'S MENU
For Children 7 Years of Age and Under
CHILD'S DELIGHT
Hamburger Steak on Bun with
French Fries, Sliced Tomato,
Milk or Chocolate Milk, Sherbet
$1.00
APACHE SPECIAL
One-Quarter Fried Chicken
French Fries, Vegetable, Roll and Butter
Milk or Chocolate Milk, Sherbet
$1.00

LARGE CHEF'S SALAD
Cold Crisp Greens Topped with
Ham, Cheese, Turkey, Tomatoes,
Egg and Served with
Bleu Cheese or
1000 Island Dressing
95c

CRISP SALADS

Shrimp Louie	1.60	Crab Louie	1.70
Tomatoes Stuffed with Tuna			95c
Tomatoes Stuffed with Chicken Salad			95c
Pineapple and Cottage Cheese			95c
California Fruit Salad			95c
Combination Sea Food Salad			1.80
Tossed Green Small Salad			40c
French Fries			25c
Potato Salad (side)			35c
Macaroni Salad (side)			35c

PASTRIES

Cream Pie 30c		Flaky Crust Pie	25c
	A la Mode (Extra) 10c		
Jell-O 25c		Cake	25c

A LA CARTE

CHOICE NEW YORK STEAK	2.50
10 Ounces	
Vegetable, French Fries and Salad	
ROAST SIRLOIN OF BEEF	1.65
Vegetable and Potatoes	
CHOICE BAKED HAM STEAK	1.65
Hawaiian Pineapple, French Fries	
SOUTHERN FRIED CHICKEN	1.50
Giblet Gravy, Vegetable and Potatoes	
Salad From Salad Bar 75c Extra	
Meat Balls with Spaghetti	1.25
Spaghetti with Meat Sauce	85c
Veal Scaloppini, Mushrooms	1.50

FOUNTAIN

Milk Shakes	35c
Malts	40c
Sodas	35c
Tiny Tot Sundae	25c
All Sundaes	40c
Ice Cream	15c-25c
Sherbet	15c-25c
Root Beer	15c-25c
Pepsi	15c-25c
Root Beer Float	30c
No Substitutes, Please	

OPEN 24 HOURS -- 7 DAYS

APPETIZERS

Mixed Sea Food Cocktail	95c
Crab or Shrimp Cocktail Small	60c
Crab or Shrimp Cocktail Large	95c
California Fruit Cocktail	35c
Mix. Gr. Salad (Choice of Dressing)	40c
Soup du Jour	25c

COMPLETE DINNERS
Includes Salad from Our Salad Bar,
and Soup de Jour — Coffee and Dessert

APACHE SPECIAL $3.50
T-BONE STEAK
Includes Salad from Our Salad Bar,
Coffee and Dessert

CHOICE TOP SIRLOIN STEAK	3.50
CHOICE N.Y. CUT STEAK	3.95
FILET MIGNON	4.00
CHOPPED ROUND STEAK	1.95
VEAL CUTLET, Country Gravy	1.95
VEAL SCALOPPINI	2.25
with Mushrooms	
CHICKEN FRIED STEAK	2.25
SOUTHERN FRIED CHICKEN	2.25
BAKED N.Y. CUT STEAK	4.25
(for two)	8.00

BEVERAGES

Coffee 10c Tea 15c Iced Tea 15c Milk 15c

BOWLER'S SPECIAL
½ Pound Ground Beef with
French Fries
or Potato Salad
85c

Its the Same Fine Food and Service Whether You Eat In The Apache Dining Room Or In The Coffee Shop

APACHE DINING ROOM & COFFEE SHOP

2030 TEXAS STREET .... FAIRFIELD 425-8385

The Apache Dining Room & Coffee Shop menu. *Fairfield Civic Center Library microfilm.*

scaloppini, filet of sole, Lobster Thermidor, hot sandwiches, milkshakes, chili dogs, pastries à la carte and more. It even had French-fried frog legs.

Two years later, it became Ernie's Steak House, with the new management team of Ernie and Dottie Sousa. The menu consisted of "the finest eastern beef and Australian lobster tail." Patrons could select their own steak that was then "deliciously cooked on our famous char-glow broiler."

Sousa owned the bowling alley until its demise. It wasn't the quality of the food that hastened the end, it was the crime and drugs that had taken over the bowling alley. As part of a redevelopment deal, Sousa sold it to the city of Fairfield so a United States Postal Service (USPS) office could be constructed on the site. However, the USPS fell on hard times after the sale, and the proposed post office never came to be. The bowling alley was demolished in 2002, and the old location sat vacant for two decades. Finally in 2022, construction began on a new community center focused on programming for youth.

SMORGA BOB'S: FAIRFIELDERS GET THEIR GRUB ON

All. You. Can. Eat.

Evidently, for many Fairfielders, those four words are akin to hearing your favorite song on the radio. The lineage of local put-the-feedbag-on restaurants runs from Gam's (which preceded Happy Steak on Oak Street) to JJ North's and continues to Hometown Buffet. But the bygone restaurant most associated with stuffing your face is definitely Smorga Bob's, which used to be located at 1720 West Texas Street and opened in 1968.

A not-scientific-but-still-interesting poll that offered over fifty choices in the ten-thousand member "I Grew Up in Fairfield, Too" Facebook group asked which former Fairfield restaurant locals missed the most. The results showed convincingly that Smorga Bob's was the favorite.

Sometimes, less is more—but sometimes, more is more.

The following is a partial list of what many Fairfielders chowed down on over the years: barbecued ribs, batter-fried fish, collard greens, fried potatoes, egg foo young, chicken chow mein, cracked Alaskan crab, grilled liver and onions, corned beef and cabbage, baked meatloaf, chicken fried steak, baked lasagna, London broil, Cornish game hens, oysters, salmon, scallops, sautéed mushrooms, baked potatoes, beef burgundy, rainbow trout, noodles almondine, fried clams, sliced watermelon, peach cobbler, fruit ambrosia, buttered egg noodles, tacos and much more. Whew!

Smorga Bob's Family Restaurant is where Fairfielders went to get their grub on—and sometimes pilfer the fried chicken. *Armijo High yearbook, 1977.*

But hands down, the two items that most old-timers associate with Smorga Bob's were its crispy fried chicken and (cue the Hallelujah chorus) soft serve ice cream.

The "Bob" in Smorga Bob's referred to Robert H. White from Sacramento. Along with his partner, Richard "Dick" Wheeler, he opened the first Smorga Bob's in Woodland in 1967.

White had owned a twenty-four-hour coffee shop in West Sacramento and thought that a smorgasbord-style eatery could be very lucrative. In 1966, he sought investors to buy into his idea and almost had them before they backed out. He then convinced Wheeler to invest in converting a failing Woodland restaurant called Jack in the Beanstalk into his vision. They were given an offer they couldn't refuse: they could walk away from the investment at any time with just a thirty-day notice.

The business plan was to offer an all-you-can-eat dinner for only $1.49. It was a ploy that could only work in their favor if they brought in a large volume of customers. They did. Within sixty days, they doubled their business, and thirty days after that, they tripled it. They were aided by an advertising blitz that included newspaper and radio advertisements, placards and billboards.

In September 1967, they introduced the Make-Your-Own-Sundae, which was a huge success. The original investors who had balked before suddenly reappeared just in time for the birth of the second Smorga Bob's, located in West Sacramento, to be born.

Fairfield's Smorga Bob's was the third and opened in 1968. It was the first to be built from the ground up as opposed to being converted from an existing restaurant. Even though its location on West Texas Street was in the slower part of town, it was an immediate local hit.

Eventually, the chain of highly successful Smorga Bob's Family Restaurants consisted of eight franchises, including shops in Napa, Livermore, Roseville, Concord and Vallejo.

When asked about how Smorga Bob's could offer so much to eat at such low prices, in a 1976 interview Robert White explained that they merely traded off employee costs and food costs. With the smorgasbord format, only a fraction of the many kitchen helpers and waitresses employed by

Smorga Bob's advertisement from the 1970s. *Fairfield Civic Center Library microfilm.*

other restaurants were needed. Also, they were open only during the peak lunch and dinner hours. That way, they were able to translate the money saved on extra employees into more food on customer's plates.

White estimated that the average eater at his establishments ate 25 to 50 percent more food than they would at an ordinary restaurant. A little-known fact is that Smorga Bob's provided the food for the Elderly Nutrition Program in three counties.

At the early Smorga Bob's, before they hired dedicated store managers, Bob White was in charge of all the food components and Dick Wheeler was in charge of what is now called human resources. Walt Geer, a certified public accountant, handled all the finances.

According to Kirsten McFall, Geer's daughter, her father was born in Kansas in 1925 and moved with his family to Corning, California, during the Great Depression to escape the Dust Bowl. McFall's grandfather Lloyd Geer always found a way to make a living by providing food to folks and passed his restaurant knowhow down to her father.

Longtime Fairfielder Edward George Lockhart used to work at Smorga Bob's with his father, Edward Paul Lockhart, who started as fry cook there and worked his way up to become manager. "From junior high to high school, I would go to work with dad and cook food for the people of Fairfield. My dad gave me a chef's hat and an oversized chef's jacket, and I would slice meat for people in line from the Baron of Beef. I grew up hanging out with my dad at Smorga Bob's. His ultimate dad joke he used was, 'Two Eds are better than one.'"

The younger Lockhart recalled happy memories of the workers often being allowed to take home leftovers at the end of the day. He also remembered one rather traumatic incident working there:

> It was my first kitchen accident. My dad had some guys cutting zucchinis using a Chinese cleaver. He gave me a French knife and showed me how to use it. So, I was looking at those guys with the Chinese cleavers, and they're like **Whack! Whack! Whack!** with them, and I wanted to be cool like them, too. So, I got through about half of the box I was working on, and I went and got a Chinese cleaver. I was cutting, and all of a sudden **Whack!** I hit my finger. I could see it was bad. I wrapped a rag around it and showed my dad, and he said I just fell apart. My dad took a piece of dry ice from the deep freezer, burned it closed, wrapped it up and then he made me finish working! When we got home, my mom asked what happened to my hand, and my dad told her, and she made him take

me to see Dr. Hovde. He looked at it, and it didn't need stitches, and there was blood flowing there. I had no feeling in it for a long time, but it healed, and I've still got it!

Over the years, Edward George Lockhart has enhanced the culinary skills he first learned at Smorga Bob's. While he sometimes caters weddings and graduation parties, his main outlet for flexing his cooking muscles is the weekly community meal for those in need at First Baptist Church in Fairfield that he has been involved with for over two decades. He likens it to the Food Network's chef competition reality show *Chopped*. They order basic ingredients, receive a lot from the food bank, and then figure out what they're going to create with the ingredients. Although the circumstances are different, Lockhart is still cooking food for Fairfielders.

When it comes to former patrons, there were some who liked Smorga Bob's, some who loathed it, many who loved it and evidently quite a few who loved it so much they stole from it:

Linda Ueki Absher: For about a year, we went to Smorga Bob's weekly for fried chicken night, which I dreaded. Why? Because my mom, who was five feet, two inches tall and 110 pounds, would inhale enormous amounts of chicken (and the appropriate sides) and not gain a pound. Then after she was done, she would fill another plate, pull handfuls of napkins out of the container and insist that I wrap as many pieces as I could and stuff them in my purse. We'd go 'round and 'round on this, but she always won, and I wound up going to school with a purse that smelled like fried chicken.

Kelvin Wade: I'm surprised me and my family didn't eat them out of business after the first time we went there. We went back a LOT. They lost money on us. I'm surprised that when they saw us come walking up to the door they didn't quickly flip the OPEN sign to CLOSED.

Nicholas Neidlinger: One time, my brother Michael brought the whole bowl of olives to the table!

Fran Burke: I worked at Smorga Bob's for about thirty minutes! When they showed me how to transfer Jell-O into the serving tray—pick it up bare-handed and put into the tray—I quit.

Cheryl Hoskins: I would take my husband's grandmother there weekly on rib night. She loved their ribs, which I remember, they had very little meat—basically sauce on bones. She ate very little there and would bring baggies and fill them up. They saw her but never said a word.

Vicky Valentine Proud: Their mashed potatoes were like wallpaper paste. Lumpy, gritty, and sticky—all together gross. Maybe spackle might be a better description.

Tony Wade: All-you-can-eat ice cream really meant all-your-mom-will-allow-you-to-eat ice cream.

Sherri ThornGreen: My mother demanded that we learn manners, and that's where she'd take us to see how well we did. I thought it was a great buffet restaurant for families. It was clean, and the food tasted great.

Jason Britt: My family went there every Easter. One year, I grabbed liver on accident, thinking it a steak. I was soooooo excited to be able to have steak, because that wasn't something our parents let us eat. I sure was disappointed to bite into that liver. I must have been seven or eight, but I remember it like yesterday.

Cynthia Simpson: Ironically, my mom and I went there after Weight Watchers meetings.

Carl Lamera: How Smorga Bob's ever stayed in business is beyond me. It sounds like every mom was stuffing her purse and her daughter's purses with chicken, mashed potatoes and gravy.

INTERLUDE: FICTIONAL YELP REVIEWS

Yelp, the online crowd-sourcing review site where patrons can give reviews of goods and services, now has over 200 million individual reviews. Since it was founded in 2004, many of the restaurants featured in this book were obviously not reviewed on Yelp. But it made me think: what if they were?

The following fictional reviews are all negative. I could have made up some glowing ones, but where's the fun in that?

Mortimer S. Suisun City, CA
Loren's Fountain ★ ★ ☆ ☆ ☆ 8/3/1966

The whole time the lady behind the counter is scooping up my ice cream cone, I'm giving her the stink eye. When she tries to hand it to me, I refuse. I told her I had asked for the biggest cone they had. She said the triple cone was the biggest. I walked her outside and pointed to the sign with the huge cone out front and said that's what I wanted. FALSE ADVERTISING!

Jesse P. Fairfield, CA
Smorga Bob's ★ ☆ ☆ ☆ ☆ 7/16/1975

So as I'm leaving Smorga Bob's, the waiter dude stops me like he's Mannix or something and says that he saw me wrap up some chicken in foil and stick it in my pocket. I pull it out and say "Yeah, I did that." But it was chicken I had already put on my plate, not from the serving trays. He made me throw it away, which was a real waste, and I said I did not appreciate being treated like a thief. I did make it out with three drumsticks in one sock and four wings in the other, by the way.

Mortimer S. Suisun City, CA
The Black Swan ★ ☆ ☆ ☆ ☆ 3/17/1947

They will never see me here again! I came in, sat down, looked at the menu and guess what? They don't serve black swan! Not fried, grilled, boiled—nada! FALSE ADVERTISING!

Esperanza J. Fairfield, CA
Dave's Giant Hamburgers ★ ★ ★ ☆ ☆ 11/17/1964

I used to go to this same spot back in 1959–62, when I went to Armijo and when it was called Ronny's, then the Drive-In and then ¼ lb. Big Burgers. You know what they all had that this upstart Dave's doesn't? FRENCH FRIES! What kind of burger place doesn't sell fries? This place will never last!

A 1962 ¼ lb. Big Burger advertisement. It used to be where Dave's Giant Hamburger is now located. *Fairfield Civic Center Library microfilm.*

Josephine P. Fairfield, CA
Dari-Delite ★ ★ ★ ★ ☆ 10/16/1964

I am an English teacher at a local school, and while my dining experience was quite satisfactory, I did have an issue that I wanted to address. I didn't want to make a scene and also the manager was not in at the moment, so I wrote them a nice letter. I explained my considerable displeasure at the spelling of the restaurant's name. Surely, it would not have been a major inconvenience to have spelled it correctly as "Dairy Delight" instead of using made up words. This trend has gained steam, I'm afraid. From teenagers screaming and passing out at concerts by English rock bands that misspell the names of insects to "drive-thrus and do-nuts." The manager replied to my letter with her own. It used "your" instead of "you're." I shan't be going back.

Billy B. Fairfield, CA
Johanne's Hot Dogs ★ ☆ ☆ ☆ ☆ 5/5/1973

I heard that if you hit a home run at a Little League game across the street at Allan Witt Park, Johanne's would give you a free hot dog. Well, I hit a triple, so shouldn't I get three-quarters of a free hot dog? They said no.

Rocko F. San Quentin, CA
Octo-Inn ★ ☆ ☆ ☆ ☆ 3/22/1948

I went to rob the Octo-Inn and had to wait in line while two sets of other crooks were robbing it! Can't they add a take-a-number system or something?

4
Ethnic Eateries

A good restaurant just makes me giddy. I can go all day with anticipation just knowing where I'm going to eat. Sometimes, it's well-planned, sometimes it's spontaneous. Either way works.
—TV personality Gayle King

In Solano County's seat there has always been a hunger for different cuisines from around the globe, and over the years, offerings have included Mexican (Chapala, the Limit in Suisun City, Los Amigos Restaurant), Chinese (Birdcage Wok, Quan's Patio, the New China Café, the Pagoda, the

Quan's advertisement from 1958.
Fairfield Civic Center Library microfilm.

Palace Grill), Japanese (Omodaka, Sam's Teriyaki, Tasuke in Suisun City), Filipino (Green Apple), Italian (Vittorio's, Bertola's in the Fairfield Bowl, Bella Delicatessen & Pizzeria), soul food (Southern Delight, Soul Kitchen in Suisun City) and more.

This chapter highlights just a handful of diverse restaurants that the equally diverse citizens of Fairfield remember.

ETHNIC EATERIES: MEXICAN

The Hut: Mexican Food Cooked by a Swedish Man Married to a Japanese Woman

Native Nebraskan Gustave Edwin Stevens hated his Swedish birth name. His family called him Pete, his grandmother called him Steve, but all of his friends knew him as Tiny. His nickname was probably first meant jokingly, as he was a mountain of a man.

According to his granddaughter Shari Stevens, Tiny ran away from his Nebraska home when he was just fourteen years old, lied about his age and joined the U.S. Navy. He became a culinary chef and went all over the world as a seaman.

His global travels took him to Japan, where he met Yae Micki Masukawa, and they were married in 1956. Tiny came back to the states and started The Hut in 1959 at 2027 North Texas Street next to Hawkes Welding and later sent for Micki.

The Hut was probably best described as a Mexican greasy spoon restaurant, with the emphasis on greasy. Locals loved their tacos and enchiladas, and the small storefront shop was a lunch and dinner staple for decades. In 1968, the Stevenses also became the owners of Mr. Ed's across town (see chapter 6, "Reincarnated Restaurants").

Tiny and Micki were divorced in 1970 but remained business partners.

Later in life, Tiny had health problems and had to have a triple bypass. After he had another heart attack, Micki ran the restaurant by herself full time.

While Tiny and Micki owned and operated The Hut business, they did not own the land it was on. That belonged to Ray Hawkes, and in 1988, he needed it, and Micki was forced to close down.

Micki Stevens, a co-owner of The Hut, in front of the North Texas Street restaurant. *Courtesy of Shari Stevens.*

Tiny moved to a veteran's home in Nebraska, where he died in 2005. Micki passed away four years later. On Tiny's tombstone, it lists his service in both the U.S. Navy and the Air Force and includes that he was "A Very Friendly and Funny Man."

Fairfielders posted their memories of The Hut on Facebook:

Linda Huffman: I went there every Friday night while pregnant with my first daughter and left with heartburn, but it was worth it.

Tom Lish: Me and my buddy Russ Lee used to go there all the time. I think tacos were fifty cents, and you could have a good lunch for under two bucks. Remember the sign there that said, "If you want credit, go to Helen Wait?"

Karl Heins: I went there a lot when I worked at Hawkes Welding. I loved the tacos, even though they came in a bag with an inch of floating grease.

Tiny Stevens, a co-owner of The Hut, holding Tonya Taylor. *Courtesy of Teresa Taylor Courtemanche.*

Allen Wheeler: I have never had a taco since that matched the Hut's. I would walk next door from the Americana Theaters and grab one of those delicious, stain-your-shirt, heavenly treats every day.

Marylou Springer: If you asked him, Tiny would put a fried egg on the enchiladas. The place didn't look that great, but it was clean and had the best Mexican food.

Shari Stevens: It feels so good to hear just how many people remember and loved the food there. My grandparents were the best people I've ever known. They were hard workers and loved what they did. My grandma was still cooking tacos and Spanish rice for anyone who was hungry. She'd feed the whole neighborhood. She couldn't stand the fact that she was forced to retire due to property issues. She loved that place and opened up rain or shine. They only took off Sundays and Thanksgiving!

Don Clarke: The Hut was a fixture in Fairfield for years and was famous all the way to the East Coast. I was talking to a guy where I live now in North Carolina, and long story short, he knew of The Hut and asked if there was a way to get some of their hot sauce!

DAN & RUTH'S CAFÉ: SETTING THE STANDARD

Dan and Ruth Amarillas, the namesakes of the beloved Rockville Road restaurant. *Courtesy of Blanca Piedra.*

Daniel and Ruth Amarillas were naturalized American citizens, having emigrated from Mexico. They brought with them a hard work ethic and a fierce determination to succeed. When they first came to Solano County, they picked fruit and lived in a little shack, but Daniel promised his bride that he would one day get her a restaurant. He kept that promise when, together, they opened Dan & Ruth's Café on Rockville Road in the 1950s.

They built the restaurant and an adjacent home. That way, Ruth could work at the restaurant and take care of their special-needs son, William.

The chile rellenos, tacos, chile verde con carne, tamales and other dishes the restaurant served were authentic and soon became the standard by which all other local Mexican restaurant fare was measured.

Fairfielders shared spicy memories of Dan & Ruth's:

Mick McGee: The best Mexican food. We hardly ever ate out, so when Dad said we were going to Dan & Ruth's, we dropped everything to get in the car, or he'd leave without us.

Dave Boles: I ate many lunches there when I was in a rock band called Peter Sunshine. We practiced across the road in the orchard at Rick Lowe's. Must have been about '68 or '69.

Rick Laughlin: Remember the tables? They had abalone shells inlaid in them if I'm remembering correctly.

A commissioned painting of the Dan & Ruth's sign by artist Donna Covey. *Donna Covey Paintings.*

Leann Lytle: As kids, we loved it when Mom and Dad would let us buy the candy at the register. The boxes of French burnt peanuts and Boston baked beans were my faves. How do I remember that?

Shari Welsh Rutter: Dan & Ruth's is the Mexican food I grew up on and the Mexican food I judge all others by!

Dale Stump: It was a great place to have breakfast after hunting up on Twin Sisters.

Claudette Ramirez: Dan and Ruth were my great-uncle and great-aunt. I remember going there all the time, and they had those old-fashioned Homer Laughlin dishes with branding irons and steers heads on them. I remember climbing trees, picking fruit from the fruit trees there, and my great-aunt, we called her Cuca, teaching me how to cook chile rellenos. I need to say that I believe that they would not have had what they did if not for Cuca. She was very financially savvy. She loaned my dad money when he first started getting going in business because she had it. She was very smart and very strong.

ETHNIC EATERIES: ITALIAN

Rockville Inn

Rockville Inn (also known over the years as Rockville Corner, Rockville Corner Inn, Rockville Café and Bar, Rockville Tavern & Restaurant and the Rockville Bar and Grill) qualifies as an ethnic eatery in two different iterations: first as an Italian restaurant and later as a Japanese restaurant.

The building, still standing in 2022, is a historical landmark that was built around 1915 and was the station stop for the Sacramento Stagecoach Route. It became a general store that was used for decades by residents of the old township of Rockville and its municipal descendants. In February 1947, Veraldo "Marty" Muratori and his wife, Amelia, opened a new store, tavern and restaurant in the historic structure. The Muratoris owned the business block and leased to other businesses, including York's meat market, a barbershop and Paul's cleaners.

The new Italian restaurant was housed in the space formerly used for the store and didn't have its official grand opening until May 3, but it soon became the local go-to spot for authentic Italian cuisine.

In 1949, it added the Blue Room and cocktail lounge, which was completely redecorated with a new bar, wall and floor coverings.

Judy Baucom poses by the Rockville Corner–mobile (not the official name). *Armijo High yearbook, 1962.*

In 1959, Bill and Elaine Cloud and Shirley and Pete Baucom took over management of the Rockville Corner and had their grand opening in September. Their Western Room featured covered wagon décor and the addition of an innovation that was becoming more and more ubiquitous in America: a television.

The menu featured twenty-three items to choose from, including New York steak, prime rib, poultry, seafood and much more. In 1960, the restaurant started Monday night family spaghetti dinners, complete with soup, salad, an entrée, dessert and coffee for one dollar per person.

Keeping a local link to the land was important. A 1963 advertisement touted a prize red Angus steer that would be served that weekend. It had been purchased at the Solano County Fair junior auction from the Suisun Valley 4-H Club. It also served wines from the Suisun and Napa Valleys.

In early 1976, the Futami Inc. Corporation took over the management of the Rockville Corner Inn and began serving Japanese and American dishes. The waitresses wore kimonos, and the menu included tempura, chicken teriyaki, top sirloin teriyaki, sukiyaki and sushi.

Tamer Totah began working at the Rockville Bar & Grill in 1989, when he was nineteen years old. His father and uncle started the business, and Tamer bought it in the mid-1990s. He served typical American fare at first but decided to change the menu to Italian, returning full circle to where it had started with the Muratoris.

Locals shared memories of the Rockville Corner Inn:

Dan Monez: It was a big treat for my dad to take us there for Mrs. Muratori's wonderful Italian cooking. I especially remember her thick minestrone soup served family style in a huge tureen with lots of parmesan. Her ravioli was also my personal favorite. Sometimes in the summer, when we had the fruit stand and ranch (where the red Ice House building is), we would get to have a hamburger from there for lunch. Yum!

Chuck Patton: I fell for the "Alaskan fur fish" story that the bartender told me. It was a fake fish covered with fur, probably made by a taxidermist as a joke, like a jackalope.

Jerry Noble: I really liked that place. I remember there was a picture of a grizzly bear on the wall that they said was shot in the vicinity of Rockville Park during the 1800s.

Mike Venning: I had my first drink at a bar there. Since the statute of limitations has expired, I was fifteen at the time.

PIETRO'S

Pietro Murdaca was born in Antonimina, Italy, and came to Vacaville in 1956 with his wife, Amalia, and their three children. The following year, he opened a small restaurant in Vacaville and introduced the California North Bay Area to authentic Southern Italian cuisine.

After the success of their first restaurant, Pietro's No. 2 (also in Vacaville) came along five years later. The Fairfield Pietro's was launched in 1978 at 711 Madison Street (in 2022, the home of Chez Soul), and despite numerous Fairfielders holding it in high esteem in their memories, evidently they didn't esteem it enough with their wallets at the time, as it closed decades ago. Both Vacaville locations continue to be Solano County favorites.

Pietro's Italian Restaurant, whose closure still saddens longtimers who look back on its remarkable food. *Armijo High yearbook, 1978.*

According to locals who worked at the Fairfield Pietro's, everything was made from scratch, including the fettucine, lasagna, steak sandwiches with meat that had been marinated in sherry, red wine and olive oil and, of course, the hand-tossed pizzas.

Robert Bright: Ah, Pietro's…my dad had a pizza named after him there, and they made it to precision. I miss that place.

Carl Lamera: Pietro's was the first pizza I had with a thick crust. It was like dessert when you got to the end of the pizza, swiped the crust with a pat of butter and let it melt.

ETHNIC EATERIES: CHINESE

Eastern Café

Over the years, a number of Fairfielders have posted in the "I Grew Up in Fairfield, Too" Facebook group about the rather ramshackle husk of a building (still there in 2022) that used to be the Eastern Café. Some cannot remember ever seeing it open, while others definitely recall eating there.

Veronica Anne Hale: It's always bugged me that it has been empty since at least 1989. I know because that's when I used to not deliver mail there when I had that route.

Shar Stewart: Inside, it's still set up as if it was to open, but it never does…maybe it's haunted!

Eastern Café was owned by longtime Fairfielders George and Pearl Young. The original site was 2045 North Texas Street, where its next-door neighbor, Wendy's, now does business. It opened in 1954 and featured Chinese and American food, including chop suey, special rice dishes and fresh prawns brought in from the Bay Area.

Eastern Café was one of the oldest local Chinese restaurants, being preceded by the New China Café in Suisun City, which was around at least in the 1940s. The Youngs' restaurant also had a contemporary competitor in Quan's, which was located at 2155 North Texas Street (in the spot that the Pagoda Restaurant later occupied). Eastern Café moved to its current spot in 1967.

Gauging just how good or bad a bygone restaurant was is tricky, because good memories are often slathered with nostalgia and bad ones drizzled with bitterness. So, with that said, the following are Facebook posts about Eastern Café that (sort of) serve as Yelp reviews.

Billie D. Holland: They had the best egg rolls ever. George always made you feel like family.

William Paulos: They'd let me go behind the counter to get fortune cookies. Mom and Dad loved that place.

Cheryl Sisk Zink: I worked there for two hours. I couldn't work for the owner, she was mean…but I was meaner. It didn't end well for her. She wore the soda I was drinking as I walked out the door.

Mark Caudill: Like all fine Chinese restaurants, it had a quiet, peaceful atmosphere, so relaxing for fine dining.

Eastern Café back in its heyday. *Armijo High yearbook, 1975.*

Hope Williams: I got sick from eating there just before they closed.

Rebeckah Shurrum: I used to work there. The owners loved to fight and throw things at each other. They fired me a few times! I was only thirteen.

Diane Lynn Baranik: I was just a little munchkin, about four years old, and I remember my first fried shrimp—I fell in love!

The remains of Eastern Café in 2020. *Courtesy of Tony Wade.*

Even though it was located on North Texas Street, a main Fairfield thoroughfare, the Eastern Café was not immune to burglars. In 1968, a thief who police later surmised must have been tiny to squeeze into a small window covered by an iron bar that had been hacksawed, made off with about $610 (over $4,800 in 2022) worth of cash and goods. The take was $150 in cash and the rest in frozen meat.

After George Young died, his wife ran the restaurant for many years until it closed. Evidently, the family still owns the land.

The decaying structure now looks every bit of its fifty-plus years and then some—especially juxtaposed with the remodeled Wendy's next door. There is a "For Rent" sign in the front window, with written instructions for potential lessees to leave their information in the mail slot.

For now, the Eastern Café remains a very visible Fairfield "ghost of dining out past."

GONE BUT NOT FORGOTTEN:
WELL, SOME ARE FORGOTTEN

The following are just a few other Fairfield restaurants that I came across in microfilm. The date listed is the date of the advertisement, not when the restaurant was founded.

A Breakfast Nook (1997) 532-A Jackson Street: omelettes, homemade biscuits and sausage gravy

Bob's Place (1962) 2035 North Texas Street: buffet

Breadmaster Sandwich Shoppe (1979) 3035 Travis Boulevard: Boston clam chowder, crab and avocado sandwiches

Chauncey's of Fairfield (1987) Winery Square, West Texas Street: steaks, seafood

Chicken Mania (1988) 1657 North Texas Street: charbroiled chicken sandwiches, chicken soup, liver pate

Chuck's Inn (1964) 1310 West Texas Street (Country Corner Shopping Center): fish and chips, southern fried chicken, roast beef sandwiches

Dodd's Restaurant (1947) one-quarter mile west of the old county hospital on Highway 40: American food

Fairfield Home Bakery and Restaurant (1912) the corner of Texas and Jackson Streets: pies, rolls, lunches, ice cream

Fresh Choice (2015) 1501 Travis Boulevard: salads, soup, baked potatoes, pasta

Fusilli Ristorante (1997) 620 Jackson Street: Italian and seafood

Green Apple (1983) Mission Village Shopping Center, 2703 North Texas Street: Filipino food, lumpia

Ken's Texas Barbecue (1978) 1957 North Texas Street: barbecued beef, chicken and pork

Kermit's Hot Dogs (1979) Mission Village Shopping Center, 2791 A North Texas Street: chili dogs, Mexican taco dogs, Italian pizza dogs

Los Amigos Restaurant (1963) 101 Union Avenue: enchiladas, tacos, tamales

Marchand's (1983) 1690 West Texas Street: fine dining

Marie Callender's (1988) 1750 Travis Boulevard: freshly baked pies

Melody Inn (1955) Highway 40, near Cordelia Junction: porterhouse steaks, wine

Milly's Giant Burger (1973) 2260 North Texas Street: burgers and hot dogs

Milly's Giant Burger was located—evidently briefly, as almost no one remembers it—in the same place as Dari-Delite/Crunchy's. *Fairfield Civic Center Library microfilm.*

Left: Sassafras Old Fashioned Ice Cream Parlor is remembered for its bubblegum ice cream and its server's uniforms. *Armijo High yearbook, 1983.*

Right: Vicki's Drive-In opened behind Colony Kitchen in 1972. *Armijo High yearbook, 1975.*

One Potato, Two Potato (1980) 3055 Travis Boulevard: baked potatoes with myriad toppings

Pete's Restaurant (1958) 1117 West Texas Street: steak, chicken

Pups on a Pole (1981) Solano Mall: corn dogs

¼ lb. Big Burger (1962) 1055 North Texas Street: burgers, fried prawns

Rax Restaurants (1985) Solano Mall: roast beef, baked potatoes

Sassafras Old Fashioned Ice Cream Parlor (1983) 900 Texas Street: ice cream sundaes, desserts

Teriyaki Kitchen (1985) 3079 Travis Boulevard: teriyaki chicken, vegetable tempura

Terminal Café (1964) 1411 West Texas Street: soup, salad, breakfast

Vegan Para-Dice (2012) 846 Texas Street: vegan sandwiches, burgers, desserts

Vicki's Drive-In (1972) 1470 Holiday Lane: burgers, burritos, steak sandwiches

Waterman Park Cafeteria (1940s) Waterman Park: American Food, steaks, fountain service

The Wooden Shoe Restaurant (1978) 624 Jackson Street: continental cuisine

5

Past Pizza Place Timeline

Pizza is like sex: when it's hot, it's great. When it's cold…still pretty good!
—*Fairfielder Bruce Gross*

M aking a pizza is not rocket science. I mean, you have the crust, you slap some tomato sauce on that bad boy, add cheese, then the rest of your toppings and bake it. Voilà! However, piecing together a past pizza place timeline—now that, my friends, is a challenge. It's not like there's a nationwide pizza database on the internet (even though there really should be).

So while some of the dates in the following chapter are exact, others (with asterisks) are best guesstimates deduced from *Daily Republic* microfilm, high school yearbooks and Polk City Directories (basically hardcover, old-school phone books). This timeline is not meant to be all-inclusive. For the most part, the establishments listed are primarily pizzerias, not other kinds of restaurants that also served pizza.

*1958: THE KEG, WEST TEXAS STREET

According to the one advertisement for this restaurant I have discovered, the Keg was located across the street from the Lucky Supermarket that opened at 1440 West Texas Street two years earlier. It offered homemade pizza and submarine and meatball sandwiches made with homemade French rolls, and the establishment featured a player piano.

*1958: JULIO'S PIZZA HOUSE, 1400 WEST TEXAS STREET

According to an advertisement, besides pizza, Julio's also offered whole fryers, ravioli and spaghetti packed in sanitary containers—would it be cheaper in unsanitary containers?

1959: RONNY'S DRIVE INN, 1055 NORTH TEXAS STREET

Ronny's was the first restaurant located where Dave's Giant Hamburgers has been since 1963. In addition to five-for-a-dollar hamburgers or hot dogs, Ronny's also offered a "pizza burger" that came complete with a root beer for thirty-five cents.

*1960: PERRY'S PIZZARINA, 1720 NORTH TEXAS STREET

Perry Rouse was the proprietor. It had Coors Light and Dark on tap. Its pizza toppings included pepperoni, sausage, mushrooms, hamburger, linguica and—sardines?

*1960: ED'S U SAVE LIQUORS, 1914 NORTH TEXAS STREET

There is a picture in the 1962 Armijo High yearbook of two young women sampling U Save's pizza, and while I try not to practice contempt prior to investigation, it's hard not to think that liquor store pizza is probably right up there with Walmart caviar.

1961: THE DRIVE INN, 1055 NORTH TEXAS STREET

When Ronny's became The Drive-Inn, it offered New York steak, steak and eggs and hamburgers and ditched the previous incarnation's pizza burger. Instead, it sold regular pizza for sixty cents and ninety-nine cents.

*1961: BOB'S PIZZA, OHIO STREET AND UNION AVENUE AT THE RAILROAD CROSSING, HALFWAY BETWEEN FAIRFIELD AND SUISUN CITY

In the lone advertisement I've come across for Bob's Pizza, it touts its offerings as "the most delicious pizza you ever ate!" Well, that may have been true, but judging from the response of old-timers who were around back then, it more accurately might be called "the most delicious pizza that almost no one remembers."

*1963: THE LIQUOR EMPORIUM AND GOURMET PANTRY, 1701 NORTH TEXAS STREET

"Gourmet" was probably a stretch, but it sold barbecue spareribs, chicken and pizza.

1965: SHAM'S PIZZA: 124 EAST TRAVIS BOULEVARD

Sham's Pizza opened next door to Holland Dairy in 1965 and offered sixteen different varieties of pizza, as well as domestic and imported beer. A sequel, Sham's Pizza Kitchen, opened in 1966 on Parker Road near Travis Air Force Base.

At Sham's Pizza's grand opening on March 12 and 13, 1965, four members of the San Francisco 49ers made appearances, including defensive end Dan Colchico, halfback Billy Kilmer, guard Mike Magac and fullback Mike Lind.

Left: Many locals still swear that Sham's Pizza was the best pizza they've ever had. *Armijo High yearbook, 1970.*

Frank Billecci: The namesake for Sham's was Leonard Ciaramitaro, who was a football hero in high school in Martinez, and they called him "Shammy." His grandfather and my grandfather were brothers. Sham tried out for the San Francisco 49ers, but he was injured. He then worked as a highway patrol dispatcher. He decided to open a pizza place in Pleasant Hill, which thrived, as many of the 49ers would go there after practice. My grandmother and mother taught his mother how to make the pizza sauce. We call it sugo *in Sicilian.*

Orlando Resendez: One of my favorite memories! The darkened tavern effect, the buffalo, the shooting gallery, the bar and who can forget the old movies? Their pizza was the best. The cheese was the stretchiest and bubbliest, while the crust was nice and crisp. Hard to find pizza like that.

1965: STRAW HAT PIZZA SUPREME, 1803 NORTH TEXAS STREET

Christy Thompson: I loved that place. Our mom would take us there on Friday nights during basketball season when our dad [legendary Fairfield High

School coach Ron Thompson] *was coaching an away game. Old movies on the pull-down screen, pepperoni pizza and a pitcher of root beer.*

Diana Lynn Paladin: Straw Hat was where I played my first game of Pong. Got my butt kicked, too.

Barbara Ann McFadden: One of my first jobs was at Straw Hat Pizza in 1973 or '74. I once refused to serve a guy his pitcher of beer until I saw all the IDs to go with the mugs. He got mad and picked up the pitcher and threw the full contents on me and stormed out, cussing. He was arrested.

1968: SHAKEY'S PIZZA PARLOR: 2281 NORTH TEXAS STREET

At its grand opening in July 1968, beer was sold in a sixty-seven-ounce pitcher for one dollar or a ten-ounce mug for twenty cents. The full name of the pizzeria was Shakey's Pizza Parlor & Ye Public House. I have no idea what those last three words mean.

Jeff Johnson: I ran my VW bug into the wall of Shakey's one afternoon! The bumper fell off, so I threw it into the back seat, and me and my girlfriend went in for lunch!

Steve Ord: Shakey's! One time my mom was at the other end of one of those long tables and asked me for an ashtray. I thought it would be cool to slide it down to her. The glass ashtray went down about halfway and slid right off and broke into a bunch of pieces on the floor.

A Shakey's Pizza Parlor "opening soon" teaser advertisement from 1968. *Fairfield Civic Center Library microfilm.*

Tanja Duncan: I was in Chula Vista years ago and actually spotted a Shakey's Pizza! I damn near burst into tears. My daughter was looking at me crazy as I flipped an illegal U-turn. I have no idea why our Shakey's closed, but seeing the one down there brought back a flood of memories.

Carl Lamera: When I was a freshman at Fairfield High, an upperclassman (to remain nameless) took me to Shakey's after a football game. I told him that I didn't have any money. He said he didn't either. When we got there, he "social butterflied" from table to table, handing me a piece of pizza from time to time. I have never been so full on pizza that I didn't pay for—well, at least up to that point.

*1972: SNAFU CAFÉ & PIZZA PARLOR, 1411 WEST TEXAS STREET

This place was probably short-lived. It must be said, though, that Snafu Café is a seriously cool name considering *snafu* is an acronym used in the military for "Situation Normal, All F———ed Up."

1975: BIG JOHN'S SUBMARINE SANDWICHES: 1807 NORTH TEXAS STREET

Tony Wade: OK, so honestly, this one is a bit of a stretch to be called a pizza place (right up there with the Ronny's Pizza Burger), but this is personal. Big John's had a pizza sub, which was basically just melted cheese, tomatoes and salami, but I loved it. I'm talkin' loved it so much, I considered starting a new religion around it.

1977: ROUND TABLE PIZZA, 321 TEXAS STREET

At the end of every episode of the 1960s cartoon *Tooter Turtle*, the title character would try to be something he wasn't (a cowboy, quarterback, pilot, et cetera) with the help of the magical Mr. Wizard, fail miserably and

Round Table—hamburgers? *Fairfield Civic Center Library microfilm.*

need to be bailed out. Mr. Wizard would then say, "Always, always I tell you, Tooter: Be just what you is, not what you is not. Folks what do this has the happiest lot." Perhaps someone should have said that to Round Table before it rolled out the inexplicable Round Table Hamburger in 1977.

> *Elizabeth Nessmith: Round Table was across the street from the tennis courts at Armijo High. It was great because (1) it was within walking distance in the time allowed for lunch and (2) you could mix your own (soft) drinks. I used to do one-third 7-Up, one-third root beer and one-third Dr. Pepper.*

1978: BURNEY'S PIZZA PUB: 124 E. TRAVIS BLVD.

Burney and Vi Bielick took over the old Sham's Pizza spot near Holland Dairy and ran their establishment for about three years. The few who do remember it do so fondly, as evidently, the Bielicks were wonderful folks. The Sandwich Factory, which was there after Burney's, has even fewer people who recall it.

A 1978 Burney's Pizza Pub advertisement. *Fairfield Civic Center Library microfilm.*

1978: ROD'S PIZZA, 3027 TRAVIS BOULEVARD (SUISUN CITY ROD'S PIZZA OPENED IN *1982)

Martin Baker: I worked there, and the owner, John, was a great guy. I loved the Taco Juan Pizza at Rod's. It had a unique crust...but I still can't tell you the secret behind it.

Victor Watson: Rod's Pizza in Suisun was our Cheers. *Our home phone number was one digit off from Rod's Pizza's, so when people mistakenly called us, I would take their "order" and give them the standard answer: "Should be ready in thirty minutes!"*

*1979: ARMADILLO PIZZA: 1230-A WESTERN STREET

While the pizzas were fresh and hot and had free delivery, one of the coolest things about Armadillo's Pizza was its logo, which appeared to be the offspring of a Volkswagen Beetle that had mated with the namesake armored mammal and looked like it came from *Mad Magazine.*

Kelvin Wade: You could get a twelve-inch cheese pizza delivered for $4.90. Fast, free delivery. I think I ate 456 of those things.

1979: RICO'S PIZZA: 2755 NORTH TEXAS STREET

Scott Morrison: Rico's had a twenty-four-inch combo called the Wagon Wheel that was close to eight pounds.

Johnny Mahoe: You had to turn it at an angle just to get it in the door!

Stevie Griffin: My son Ben used to work at Rico's Pizza. He would bring home that giant pizza—I swear, it was about three feet across. It fit perfectly in the back of my Mustang when both back seats were folded down. They made the pizza crusts fresh and threw them up and twirled them in the air. At home, Ben used to practice by twirling our dish towels in the air.

RICO'S
HOME OF THE
FAMOUS 24"
PIZZA

2755 N. Texas, Fairfield
MISSION VILLAGE SHOPPING CENTER
426-1197

72" Giant Color
TV Screen—
Hour Mon. Night Football

GYROS Food fun
for
everyone

This Coupon Good For

$ 1 OFF offer
expires
1-15-84

On The Purchase Of
A Large, Family or Party Size Pizza
OR
4 Gyro Sandwiches or 4 Dinners

One coupon Pizza Coupon
Good with purchase only

Christmas Gift Certificates
Available—Ask Us!

Cynthia Garcia: My sister Sylvia used to work at Rico's Pizza. I used to call in a fake pizza order near closing time, which I'd never pick up since I was a youngster with no driver's license. The pizza just happened to have all of my sister's favorite toppings. When the restaurant closed for the night and no one picked up the pizza, my sister got to take it home. Amazing how that worked!

A Rico's Pizza advertisement from 1983. *Fairfield Civic Center Library microfilm.*

1979: ROSCOE CAPONE'S CHICAGO STYLE PIZZA: 715-B SECOND STREET

Roscoe Capone's had whole-milk cheese and a whole-wheat crust, and its specialty was called the Large Massacre. In keeping with the Windy City mobster theme, the local softball team it sponsored was called the Hit Men.

Jack Burton: I worked at Roscoe Capone's, and it was the best pizza at the time. The owner, Pat, got his meat and sausage at the Armijo Meat Company on North Texas Street.

1981: SBARRO: SOLANO MALL

Joyce Nagel Jackson: A slice of Sbarro's pizza was about as big as my car. I loved it.

Cabral Loretta: I worked at the mall, and I only made $4.25 an hour, so when I got my paycheck, I would treat myself to Sbarro's. I thought it was a fancy restaurant.

1981: GIOVANNI'S PIZZA BY THE SLICE: SOLANO MALL

Tim Putz: Giovanni's made the best sausage rolls for that Saturday morning hangover!

*1982: ROADRUNNER PIZZA: 1230 WESTERN STREET

Roadrunner ran a clever marketing campaign in 1984 called a "Cruiser's Special" that offered two dollars off a twelve-inch pizza and three dollars off a sixteen-inch pizza between the hours of 10:00 p.m. and 1:00 a.m.

1983: CHUCK E. CHEESE PIZZA TIME THEATRE: 1027 OLIVER ROAD

Chuck Davis: Man, when they opened Chuck E. Cheese, it was like Disneyland came to Fairfield.

Janet Marlette: My hubby and I had our wedding reception there. We were blending seven kids and they were all in our wedding, so it was a great bribe for them to behave during the ceremony.

Bridgette Rangel Fargo: My kids would hide under the table when Chuck E. would come out to perform.

Chuck E. Cheese with McGruff the Crime Dog and Herby the Talking Police Car in 1983. *Tim Farmer collection.*

Karl Heins: I worked there from 1985–86. Kids were right to be scared—a six-foot-tall rat wants to play? Really?

David Hall: I stopped taking the kids there when they stopped serving beer. That was the only way I could tolerate that many snot goblins.

Bill Griffin: It was a fun, family-oriented place…with the worst pizza I've ever been subjected to.

Kathy Hess: My mom had her sixty-second birthday at Fairfield's Chuck E. Cheese. Her name was up on the board with the rest of the kids. She had a ball!

*1983: GERI-TOWNE PIZZA PARLOR: 3029 TRAVIS BOULEVARD

John Babcock: My parents owned it from '85, when I was twelve, until the mid-'90s. That's where I got my first work experience. I started washing dishes, doing prep work and then worked up to cook. We always ate pizza at work and then brought it home. I couldn't stand pizza for a while after that.

*1986: PROFESSOR'S PIZZA: 1230-D WESTERN STREET

While all its varieties of pizza didn't have academic tie-ins, Fairfield fist bumps to whomever came up with naming the granddaddy of them all "the PhD."

INTERLUDE: CITY COUNCIL ENDORSEMENTS

My younger brother Kelvin Wade has written an opinion column called "The Other Side" for the *Fairfield Daily Republic* since 1992. In 2008, he published one about a then-up-and-coming city council candidate named Matt Garcia. Kelvin had assumed that he was just some starry-eyed kid, but once he had lunch with Matt at the iconic Fairfield eatery Joe's Buffet, he was convinced Matt was the real deal, and his column reflected that.

Now, in my humor column "The Last Laugh," I jokingly wrote the next week that Kelvin's endorsement could obviously be obtained by just buying him a ginormous sandwich from Joe's. Actually, Kelvin had insisted on paying, but I never let a little thing like facts get in the way of a punchline. Anyway, I then wrote the following:

> *I am fully prepared to throw my own support behind whomever is willing to give me a free meal. In fact, I decided to make it easier for city council candidates to know up front what sort of publicity can be garnered by fillin' my belly. I created a program, which is broken up into four plans—each representing a certain level of financial commitment and which details the return on their investment.*

The Tony Wade/Fairfield City Council Candidates Gastronomical Endorsement Program

Plan #1: Fast Food Frenzy (Burger King, Jack in the Box)

This low-budget plan will net political hopefuls a brief mention in my biweekly "The Lowdown" column in Friday's Diversions section, but I can't guarantee I'll spell their names correctly. Two stipulations are that I get to keep any and all toys included with the meals and that the candidate must wear either a cardboard Burger King crown or, after we eat, dance around the lobby with Jack in the Box antenna toppers stuck on all their fingers.

Plan #2: Breakfast Of Champions (Sandy's 101 Omelettes, Babs Delta Diner, Jack & Linda's Country Café)

A little pricier because I enjoy a hearty breakfast, this plan will get candidates a mention in my weekly "Inside the Raider Nation" column on the sports page. When it comes time to pony up for the meal, the candidate will be required to write on the check next to "tip"—"brush after every meal."

Plan #3: Feedbag (Hometown Buffet, Great Wall Chinese Restaurant)

If a candidate takes me to one of my two favorite all-you-can-eat places in town, they can look forward to a dazzling write-up on this very page on a Monday morning. Of course, "The Last Laugh" may be on them if my all-you-can-get privileges get revoked (again) because of my overindulgence that voids the deal.

Plan #4: Dinner Delight (Red Lobster, Mimi's Café, Hungry Hunter)

While they have to deal with my unorthodox dining behaviors (most of which I learned from Curley of *The Three Stooges*), this plan, while the most expensive, delivers more bang for the endorsement-buying buck. Candidates who choose the Dinner Delight will be mentioned in all three of my columns, have their names temporarily tattooed on my forehead, and I will perform an original song with a "Vote for ———" chorus on cable access channel 26 with my postpunk/polka/rap/bluegrass band "The Shameless Gluttons."

Now, my Fairfield City Council Gastronomical Endorsement Program was meant to be taken simply as something funny for Fairfielders to read, which would aid in their breakfast digestion, but nevertheless, after it ran, I was actually contacted by real local politicians.

I've never been one to turn down a free meal, but I have to admit that I was rather perplexed as to why they would want to talk to me. I mean, Kelvin, I can understand, because his "The Other Side" column has tackled meaty local issues in his reasoned, intelligent and cogent style for decades. Contrast that with some of the topics I've written about:

- Getting attacked by three wild tom turkeys—the "Butterballs of Death"—on Tolenas Road.
- Declaring the correct way to install a toilet paper roll is with the paper going over, not under.
- Touting a parody song about how the waving statue of Chief Solano creeps me out because he's wearing a thong.

While I'm proud of my writings, insightful political commentary they definitely ain't.

Shortly after my column ran, Kelvin and I accepted an invitation to dine with then Vice-Mayor John Mraz; his wife, Jamie; and Councilmember Catherine Moy. We had actually met with Mraz and Matt Garcia the previous year at the Blue Frog, but the restaurant's icky name and kind of icky food tainted it, so Mimi's was an upgrade.

It was a trip to meet with members of the city council away from their usual trappings (American flags, suits, banging gavels). It's kind of like a kid who sees his teacher at the supermarket and says incredulously, "Mr. Kotter, what are *you* doing here?" as if teachers only live in the classroom.

It was fascinating to get glimpses behind the curtain of local politics. I kind of felt like one of the Fairfield movers and shakers who would meet at Voici or Mac's or H-Jay's in Suisun City. Mraz and Moy talked earnestly on several issues and, in so doing, ripped the flesh off several municipal skeletons. Kelvin and I were enthralled. While the finished kielbasa is what's served up at council meetings, the backroom butchery beforehand is somewhat messy.

Now, if you think I'm going to detail everything the two councilmembers shared, you've got another think coming. I'm not tight-lipped because they asked me to be (they didn't by the way), or because I follow the time-tested truism of "what happens in Mimi's, stays in Mimi's" or even because I have any shred of journalistic integrity.

Not even close.

As a matter of fact, I've carefully catalogued all the juicy tidbits from our sit-down in my steel-trap memory and will spill the beans to anyone who'll buy me a free lunch. I mean, journalistic integrity is a wonderful thing to possess I guess, but I'll trade mine for an au jus roast beef at Joe's Buffet in a heartbeat. That's just how I roll.

Aside from all the great banter, serious talk and sharing of stories, the coolest part of the lunch was that Mraz graciously picked up the check. This saved me and Kelvin from having to perform our well-rehearsed pantomime of pretending to reach for our wallets and insisting on paying.

I mean, had the skin of a Wade actually come in contact with an unpaid check, I believe all matter in the known universe would have simultaneously exploded.

6

Reincarnated Restaurants

When a restaurant is too popular, it starts to harm the reason you are there.
—British philosopher Alain de Botton

I t has sometimes been amusing to see a couple of Fairfielders arguing on Facebook about what old restaurants used to be where. It's even more entertaining when you realize that sometimes they're both right. That's because many a Fairfield restaurant has set up shop in the old digs of past eateries. There are several that have been reincarnated over the years, and logically, using a place that functioned as an eatery before had to be way easier and less expensive than building one from the ground up.

This list is not meant to be exhaustive, and it is quite likely that some were missed or that I have them in the wrong order, as the historical record for such things is far from complete.

By the way, I don't know if you've picked up on it or not, but I really like using the term "historical record," as if I'm engaged in discovering ancient civilizations or something. It makes me feel important.

419 TEXAS STREET

Campbell's Café and the Chateau Café

As mentioned in the first chapter of this book, the first restaurant to inhabit this spot was Campbell's Café (back then, the address was 423 Texas Street), but no living person whom I have met has heard of it, much less has memories of it. The location was popular among Armijo students when the school was located on Union Avenue and when it moved to Washington Street in the mid-twentieth century. Campbell's Café later gave way to the Chateau Café in the late 1940s and 1950s.

Mr. Ed's

In the 1960s, Mr. Ed's opened in that location and featured charbroiled hamburgers and fountain service. In 1968, Tiny and Micki Stevens, who owned The Hut on North Texas Street, became the new owners.

CHATEAU CAFE

409 North TEXAS STREET

Phone HArrison 5-9905

"24 hours everyday. Excellent Quality, Friendly Service, and Air Conditioned. Chris Chantilas, Proprietor."

Above: The Chateau Café, a popular spot across from Armijo, was also the location of other restaurants in the decades that followed. *Armijo High yearbook, 1955.*

Left: Local dignitaries at the grand opening of Mr. Ed's. *Courtesy of Bobby Weatherford.*

David's English Fish and Chips/The Mandarin Restaurant/S&L Thai

In the mid-1970s, David's English Fish and Chips, owned by David Morgan, was a mainstay at 419 Texas Street. Morgan was from "across the pond," specifically Canterbury, England, and he billed his deep-fried fare as "authentic as the bloke who fries them."

Morgan first opened a food truck that posted up right outside Travis Air Force Base's main gate on Parker Road and also ran a shop at 315 Merchant Street in Vacaville before opening the Fairfield location. When locals wanted to call ahead and order his signature product, battered prawns or deep-fried frog legs, they could dial 422-3474, or 422-FISH.

In 1979, the Mandarin opened in the spot before moving to a much larger building at 219 Texas Street. Later S.&L. Thai took over.

For a couple of decades now, 419 Texas Street has just been part of a parking lot for Solano County vehicles.

Nanciann Gregg: The Chateau Café had quite a reputation when I was in school in the 1950s. Before school, there would be a thick fog of cigarette smoke in there. It was rumored that some of the girls were posing either nude or somewhat nude for a photographer upstairs. I don't know if that was true or not, but that was the rumor.

Tracy Vest: It was before my time, but I probably would never have eaten at a burger joint named Mr. Ed's. I would think they were serving a talking horse.

Jessica Duncan: Two of the Zodiac Killer's victims went to the Mr. Ed's in Vallejo before getting killed on July 4, 1969. Sorry, probably TMI.

Sandy Devlin: David's were the best fish and chips ever, and they even served ginger beer.

Tamara Beck Watson: My husband and I fell in love over David's clam strips. What more can I say?

Rick Williams: I loved that place as a kid and was sad when it closed. The first time I went there and got fries when I was expecting chips, my dad explained to me that's what they call fries in England. I thought it was the coolest thing ever. Yes, I was a dork.

David's English Fish and Chips

"As Authentic as the Bloke Who Fries Them"

Open Daily • Closed Sunday
11:30 A.M. to 8 P.M.

Menu

(DINNER INCLUDES COLE SLAW AND MUFFIN)

	a la carte	Dinner
English Fish and Chips	1.25	1.60
Battered Shrimp *SCALLOPS*	1.85	2.20
~~Battered Mini Lobster Tails~~	1.85	2.20
Fried Clams	1.40	1.75
Combination (Fish, Shrimp, ~~Lobster~~ *Scallops*, Clams)		2.90

(Scotchmans)

One Piece Fish, Chips and Cole Slaw	1.10	
~~English Pork Pie~~	.95	
English Muffin Burger	.80	

Coffee .15   English Tea .20   Milk .15

Soft Drinks (Cola, Root Beer, Orange, Wink) .25

Ginger Beer .30

315 MERCHANT ST. • Vacaville

FOR ORDERS TO GO — 448-8560

DAVID MORGAN, Esq., Proprietor

David's English Fish and Chips menu from the Vacaville location. *Courtesy of Olwyn Olly Morgan.*

150 ACACIA STREET

The Acacia

The Acacia opened in 1965 on 150 Acacia Street, and its menu included American food items, such as roast chicken, baked ham, roast beef, charbroiled steaks and family-style Italian dinners. While not a huge building, it featured a nightclub, cocktail lounge and dancing.

The restaurant evidently evolved (or devolved, depending on who is looking at it) quickly because while it had a Mother's Day special the following year, by 1968, it featured go-go dancers and a special appearance by beehive hairdo-sporting Topless Tosha, who performed (obviously) bare-breasted with a trained python.

The Office

Around 1974, the Office opened there with seafood, chicken, steaks, cocktails and live country/western music and dancing nightly. The name allowed spouses to call home and say both honestly and deceitfully that they had to "stay late at the Office."

The Abbey

The Abbey opened in the same location in the early 1970s and featured family gourmet dining items, including top sirloin, veal cordon bleu, southern fried chicken, stuffed pork chops and filet mignon. When, on July 15, 1978, the Abbey called it quits, it had a local band called the Blackwood Article do a swan-song show.

Merlyn's And Johnnie's House of Ribs

Four days after the Abbey shut down, 150 Acacia became the new home of Merlyn's. In addition to having dinner performances by a group called Windfall, it introduced its chef Johnnie Washington.

An advertisement for the occasion listed some of Washington's accomplishments, including having cooked on every continent, prepared

An advertisement that announced the opening of Merlyn's and its chef Johnnie Washington. *Fairfield Civic Center Library microfilm.*

meals for generals and jazz great Louis Armstrong, having been the chef for the Miss America Beauty Pageant and cooked for President Lyndon B. Johnson on Air Force One.

Actually, according to Washington's oldest son, James Washington, they were underselling his résumé.

My dad was in the Air Force, and his main job was the general's aide on all the bases we lived on. He had cooked for Dwight Eisenhower and John F. Kennedy, as well as Johnson. When he was stationed at Hamilton Air Force Base [in Novato, California], *Kennedy came there with his entourage, and he was associated with several movie stars* [Peter Lawford and Marilyn Monroe]. *When they tasted my dad's food, it validated him, and that networking helped him.*

While proximity to the rich, famous and powerful may have been intoxicating to some, James Washington recalled that meeting Kennedy with his father was rather painful.

That morning, I had patted my dog on the head and told him to be a good boy because I had to go someplace. Then my dad took me to introduce me to the president, and Kennedy did to me what I had just done to my dog. He patted me on my head. I remember being mad about that. I think my dad sensed I didn't like it because his great big hands were on my shoulders, and he squeezed them and guided me back to the table. I was very resentful and thought that the next time I saw Kennedy, I'd let him know. I remembered that when he was killed, and I felt so much shame.

In 1968, Johnnie Washington was sent to Travis Air Force Base, where he eventually retired. He had always run little restaurants and bar and grills or worked at the Green Valley Country Club, but once he retired from the military, he opened his own place called Johnnie's House of Ribs. Many locals to this day swear that the meat-falling-off-the-bone, savory, sweet ribs were the best they ever tasted.

Enjoy Your Easter Dinner

At Johnnie's House Of Ribs

Easter Sunday Hours: 12-9 p.m.
Regular Hours: Mon-Thurs 11-9
Fri-Sat 11-10
Sunday 4-9

Specialities of the House

Roast Prime Rib Of Beef
Barbequed Rack Of Lamb
Roast Leg Of Pork
Golden Fried Prawns & Oysters
Best Barbequed Ribs & Chicken
In Northern California-different Sauces

With Your Choice Of
Worlds Best Salad Bar

OUR DINNERS START AS LOW AS **$3 95**

146 Acacia St.•FAIRFIELD•425-0381
(Behind Stan Motors Dodge)

A Johnnie's House of Ribs advertisement featuring—a pig holding some ribs? *Fairfield Civic Center Library microfilm.*

The secret to Washington's ribs was all in the sauce, and since, according to James Washington, his father could not read or write, he seasoned everything he cooked by taste.

Over the years, Johnnie's House of Ribs moved to a number of different locations aside from the Acacia Street spot, including Parker Road and Texas Street.

In the Netflix streaming political thriller *House of Cards*, Kevin Spacey played a president who loved eating ribs made by an African American chef named Freddy who owned Freddy's BBQ Joint. There's no evidence that Johnnie Washington was the inspiration for the character, but he probably could have been.

Stephanie Leibowitz: That dark-brown barbecue sauce was the best I've ever had.

Bob Carver: In the early '90s a band I was in called LandShark played at Johnnie's when it was located at the end of West Texas Street where Chauncy's had been. The place was pretty wild and also featured strippers and comedy. One of the bartenders that worked there was kind of a celebrity, and his name was Bruce Bell. When we played there, I would sometimes take a very long guitar solo, and because I had a wireless system, I could get on top of the bar and play, and it would be a kind of circus act. Bruce the bartender would often pour whiskey shots down my throat while I played, and it became part of the show. One particular night, he decided to pour a double shot of Bacardi 151 down my throat instead of the normal shot of Jack. So when the 151 went down my gullet, it burned like hell, and I thought I was going to puke right there on the bar. Somehow, I kept myself together, jumped off the bar and ran to the back bathroom where I flipped the guitar over my shoulder and promptly yakked up all the contents of my stomach while the band finished the song out front without me. Everyone had a good laugh, and I never trusted Bruce again. The good old days!

1720 NORTH TEXAS STREET

Sara's Pancake House

As far as can be sussed out from microfilm and other sources, Perry's Pizzarina was the first local restaurant in this location in 1960, but the first that most local old-timers actually remember was Sara's Pancake House. It opened around 1961 and who exactly Sara was remains a mystery (to me). However, the reason many remember the popular breakfast, lunch and dinner spot is due to the efforts of the second owners who purchased the shop in 1963, Jim and Carol Bennett. Jim Bennet felt so strongly about being his own boss that he resigned from the Fairfield Police Department to become a restaurateur.

When it came to the food, Sara's had it covered. Listing some of the varieties of its titular fare brings to mind the scene in the movie *Forest Gump* where Bubba recites all the different types of shrimp he enjoyed back home. Sara's had buttermilk pancakes, buckwheat pancakes, Hawaiian pancakes,

Sara's Pancake House in the early 1960s. *Courtesy of Karen Bennett Moore.*

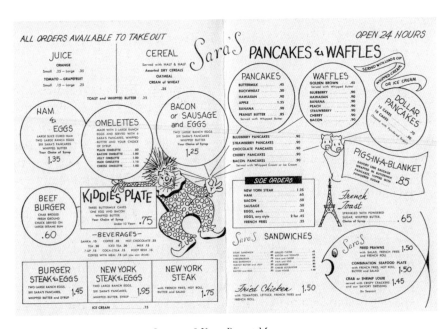

Sara's Pancake House menu. *Courtesy of Karen Bennett Moore.*

apple pancakes, banana pancakes, pancakes with blueberries, strawberries, chocolate, cherry pancakes and—wait for it—bacon pancakes.

They also served three-egg omelettes, pigs in a blanket, French toast and more. Sara's lunch and dinner entrees featured steaks, center-cut ham, fried chicken, lobster, crab and swordfish among other items.

The Bennetts expanded and adjusted the menu, and in subsequent years it went from boasting sixteen types of pancakes to seventeen, eighteen and all the way up to twenty. In 1964, the restaurant was remodeled and a banquet area was added, nearly doubling its size. The following year, Sara's No. 2 opened in Vacaville, followed by sequels in Woodland and Fort Bragg.

Karen Bennett Moore, the daughter of Carol and stepdaughter of Jim, worked at Sara's for several years and shared some recollections:

> *One of the first things they did was make it a twenty-four-hour restaurant. The counter was right in front, so people could watch their food being prepared. All the booths had little jukeboxes, and there was also one big main jukebox. At lunchtime, they had huge hamburgers that were really good. I don't know if you could compare them to Dave's, but they were huge. I remember a few different celebrities that came by like actor Victor Buono* [from What Ever Happened to Baby Jane? and Hush Hush Sweet Charlotte] *and country singer Jimmy Wakeley, who left several records.*

Sadly, by 1970, the Bennetts were delinquent on their Internal Revenue Service taxes and had to sell the restaurant. The notice in the paper listed all the separate items for sale, which had to be bought as a lot, not individually. While it included big items, like broilers and a dishwashing machine, it was very thorough. The final things listed were "1 highchair, miscellaneous silverware, dishes, salt-pepper-sugar dispensers, cooking utensils and toy stuffed animals."

Rusty's Fine Foods

Rusty's Fine Foods occupied the former Sara's spot for about four years in the mid-1970s and featured broasted chicken. Tuesdays were family night, and the special was a half chicken, salad, French fries, a roll and butter for $1.49 (in 1972).

By the way, the broasted chicken thing evidently was introduced in the Fairfield area in 1964 at, of all places, the Liquor Emporium at 1701 North Texas Street. In that year, it published a newspaper advertisement explaining the process: "Our chicken is prepared in scientific new equipment called broasters. The broaster injects heat units, instantaneously sears the chicken, seals in all flavorful natural juices and cooks through to the bone in eight minutes. Broasted chicken is served golden brown, tender and wonderfully palatable." According to Wikipedia, "The broasting technique began in 1954 when American businessman and inventor, L.A.M. Phelan combined parts of a deep fryer and pressure cooker as a way to cook chicken more quickly. Phelan trademarked the words *broaster* and *broasted food*.

To answer your thought balloon question—no, you definitely didn't need to know all that about broasting, but the available Rusty's Fine Foods informaion was only two sentences long.

David's English Fish and Chips and Nancy's

According to the 1977 Polk City Directory, David's English Fish & Chips was at least briefly located at 1720 North Texas Street. That stay was followed by a multiple-year residency by Nancy's Restaurant, although the historical record (yes, I used that term again) is fuzzy on the details.

Sunrise International Restaurant

Opening in 1980, Sunrise International Restaurant was owned and operated by 1974 Fairfield High graduate Richard Meares. It offered a variety of omelets, waffles topped with fruit, chocolate cheesecake and steak and seafood dinners. It had a sushi bar as well.

Meares cut his culinary teeth working at the Red Top Restaurant as well as right across the street at Voici. While at Voici, he learned how to create images with food and work magic with flavors from the original chef there, Cecil Villanueva. Meares also spent time at a private school in Oregon, where he created dinners for a conservatory of music and cooked for jazz luminaries like Chick Corea and Stanley Clarke. He also later catered the Senior PGA Tour.

Meares was born in Japan and came to the United States when he was eleven. At Sunrise, he started what could be called an exchange program with his aunt who lived in Tokyo. She had visited and found the omelets compelling and took the idea back to the land of the rising sun.

While his aunt rightly deduced Japanese folks would crave American omelets, Meares in turn discovered that Americans enjoyed steamed and fried rice with their hearty breakfasts and added it to the menu.

Sandy's 101 Omelettes: Everything Including the Kitchen Sink

While discovering who the Sara behind Sara's Pancakes has proved to be elusive, the Sandy behind Sandy's 101 Omelettes, which began calling that location home in 1997, is former Fairfield resident Sandy Calvert.

Calvert began working down the street decades before as a waitress at Sambo's three months after it opened in 1968. She also worked at other local eateries, including Howard Johnson's and Lyon's, and in the '80s, she opened Harbor Lights restaurant in the Suisun City Marina.

Sandy's 101 Omelettes' menu was impressive. Their three-egg omelets included everything from a plain no. 4 (bacon and cheese), to a little more

The "kitchen sink" interior of Sandy's 101 Omelettes. *Courtesy of Eric Rench.*

exotic no. 49 (linguica, spinach and sour cream), to the adventurous no. 84 (chicken livers, onions and olives). No. 101 was called the Kitchen Sink and was a six-egg omelet that included just about everything but seafood and chicken livers.

When it came to the décor, the "kitchen sink" was also an apt way to describe the theme, as nearly every bit of wall space was covered by signs, knickknacks, doodads and keepsakes of all sorts.

Grandma's Place and Raul's Striper Café 2

When Sandy closed the restaurant in 2010 and moved down North Texas Street to the former Sambo's spot, her old vendors, Bill and Phyllis Cleaver, bought it and opened up as Grandma's Place. When all of Sandy's decorations were removed, the place looked rather naked in contrast.

Grandma's Place didn't last that long and was replaced by Raul's Striper Café 2, a sequel to the original Raul's Striper Café in Rio Vista, owned by Raul and Michelle Rodriguez.

As of 2022, the restaurant at 1720 North Texas Street is Your City's Café. The current shop's menu retains nods to its predecessors by offering pancakes, waffles, fried rice and even features its own kitchen sink omelet.

2440 MARTIN RD.

Sherwood Forest

Sherwood Forest had its grand opening on April 22, 1976, at the very visible location off of I-80, near the Air Base Parkway exit close to Woodard Chevrolet. It was owned by Ernest Sousa, who had previously owned Ernie's Steak House at the Fairfield Bowl with his wife, Dottie. Years later, he was back with a new place—and a new wife, Joanne.

A sampling of the opening weekend menu, which happened to be Easter, included:

- Roast tom turkey with sage celery dressing, giblet gravy and cranberry sauce.

Above: A vintage Sherwood Forest matchbook cover. *Courtesy of Keith Hayes.*

Right: A 1976 advertisement for Sherwood Forest, featuring local performer Gussie Kolda. *Fairfield Civic Center Library microfilm.*

- Virginia baked ham with sherried fruit sauce and candied yams.
- Roast leg of lamb with mint jelly.
- Baked stuffed breast of capon with giblet gravy.
- Roast prime rib of beef au jus.
- New York cut steak with a mushroom sauté.

Prices ranged from $5.95 to $8.50 for the various entrées.

Sherwood Forest often featured local and regional live performers, including in-demand Fairfield pianist Gussie Kolda, who performed at Dick's Restaurant and many other locations.

Lord Jim's

In 1978, Lord Jim's opened in that location, added a new dance floor and kept up the tradition of having live entertainment. At one point, according to an advertisement, it featured a group called Whisper (uh, not *The* Whispers).

145

Fairfield Landing and Hungry Hunter

Fairfield Landing is probably what most locals remember at that spot. Its tagline was "The Complete Dining Experience." To back that up, it served fresh snapper, scallops, mahi mahi, teriyaki chicken, trout almondine and a special called the Union Line. The latter featured thinly sliced steak marinated in a special blend of cabernet, soy sauce, herbs and spices that was then charbroiled and topped with fresh sautéed mushrooms.

Live music and dancing were draws for locals, and many popular Fairfield bands, like Laser Boy, played there frequently.

After Fairfield Landing, the spot became Hungry Hunter, and in 1996, it was voted "Business of the Year."

Locals shared remembrances:

Melody Brute: Lots of inappropriate stuff happened when I worked at Fairfield Landing. One of the managers only had half an arm and he used to come up, wiggle his elbow at you and then touch you on your chin. He was fondly called "Freddy the one-armed bandit." It freaked out one of the other bus people, and she'd always scream and run away.

Gloria Jean Lee: They had great prime rib, and I loved watching our waiter/waitress make our salad at the table!

Clay Sharps: I was asked to leave once after getting back from the Marines. It seemed that they didn't like airmen getting knocked out in their bar. I only hit him once.

Jenny Johnson: A girlfriend and I started going to Fairfield Landing in 1982 most Friday or Saturday nights to dance. I never accepted drinks from anyone because back then, it seemed like guys thought that was an invitation for more. We used to give out wrong phone numbers to them.

In 1983, I met a guy who I danced with a lot. Our first official date was at a Halloween party there. We married that same year and have been married for over thirty-seven years. He likes to tell people he picked me up in a bar.

On the weekends, if you were not there by 9:00 p.m., you would not get a table. It was standing room only at the bar by 10:00 p.m. It was just a really nice place to go. So much fun and the people were so nice. Not like the meat market bar called BJ's.

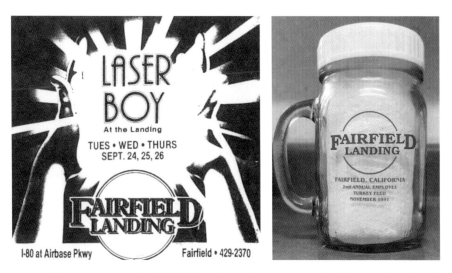

Left: A 1985 advertisement for Fairfield band Laser Boy playing at Fairfield Landing. *Fairfield Civic Center Library microfilm.*

Right: A keepsake Fairfield Landing jar. *Courtesy of Margaret Lewis.*

Hungry Hunter in 1996. *Fairfield Civic Center Library microfilm.*

Mitchell Walker: Working at Fairfield Landing was even more fun. Talk about after-parties: when the patrons were gone, the staff would let loose. Once in a while, I stayed so late, I'd sleep in my truck because I had to be back on shift in a couple of hours.

Lida Wegley: I got my fake ID taken away when I went there. Bad girl.

Dennis Tenney: I loved playing at Fairfield Landing. The stage was kind of small, but the crowds were awesome. We were told we could not come back after I climbed the pergola over the stage and played a solo from up there. They changed their minds after they totaled the week's receipts. We were back the next month.

Terri Keys: I remember going to Fairfield Landing all the time with my ex-husband. Every time he would do the Michael Jackson spin I had to duck down or I'd get a face full of Jheri curl juice!

7

Setting the Record Straight

I avoid conflict—like, any conflict—at all costs. I hate it. Even at a restaurant, if I get the wrong order, I'll just eat it anyway because I don't want to make an issue.
—American actor Robin Lord Taylor

In my first book, *Growing Up in Fairfield, California*, I explained the differences between the Fairfield Area Rapid Transit (FART) buses and the Dial-A-Ride-Transit (DART) vans that Fairfielders often confused with one another. Some were sure that the FART buses, which long ago faded into (chuckle-icious) memory, somehow became the still-used DART, but like Vinny Gambini knocking down theories with irrefutable evidence, I demonstrated that that was not accurate. (I promise that will be the last *My Cousin Vinny* reference in this book, by the way.)

In this chapter, I will attempt to set the record straight on questions concerning old-time, bygone restaurants and also include some remembrances from others.

SKATES OR NO SKATES?

More than a few Fairfielders have posted on Facebook that they recall waitresses at Sid's Drive-In and A&W Drive-In serving customers while they were zipping around on roller skates. Now, this was before my time, so I consulted longtime locals who had firsthand experience. Nanciann Gregg was a carhop at Sid's and she said they did not wear skates. She said that the doors leading out from the kitchen to the outside area were those swinging saloon types, which would have been impossible to navigate on skates when you often had to use your knee to open it while carrying two trays out to the cars.

Janelle Pritchard Hawkins, who worked at A&W, said they did not use roller skates because the blacktop was uneven. She said it had essentially been a field before it was graded, and they just poured the blacktop over it.

Cathy O'Dell, who was the first carhop Sid Withrow of Sid's hired, said they did not use roller skates.

Melody Anderson, however, worked at Sid's in 1965; it was her first job. She remembers being a carhop on skates, falling and spilling hot chocolate all over her white blouse.

Now, my suspicion is that the recollections of carhops wearing skates are a case of actual memories being woven together with ones from the TV show *Happy Days* and the movie *American Graffiti*. That said, Melody Anderson has a very specific memory of an event that, even though it happened decades ago, is the kind of thing that would stick with you.

Now, it also could be that all the former waitresses are correct, as they worked at different times. I've never come across any evidence that they were on skates at either restaurant. It would seem like that would be a thing that would be at least mentioned if it were the case. However, I am not sure, so I have to leave it there.

WAS FAIRFIELD'S ARNOLD'S FOOD THE INSPIRATION FOR ARNOLD'S ON *HAPPY DAYS*?

After selling the Black Swan, Arnold Maupin bought twenty-two acres near where the western edge of Solano Mall sits and opened a smaller eatery called Arnold's Food.

Locally, it has been rumored that the second restaurant was the inspiration for Arnold's Drive-In featured in the TV show *Happy Days*. The (sub)urban legend is that famous Fairfielder Nori "Pat" Morita, who played the namesake proprietor of Arnold's Drive-In in the ABC sitcom, once worked at Arnold's Food and told producers about it. There is no proof or truth to that. At the time Maupin was running Arnold's Food, Morita was working at his family's restaurant, Ariake Chop Suey in Sacramento.

C.&K. DRIVE-IN OR SNO-WHITE/SNO-MAN?

Now, this one is a little tricky. Old-timers have asked if anyone remembers a burger restaurant that was on Union Avenue. The answer could actually be two places. The Sno-White, which later became the Sno-Man, was located on Union Avenue and fits the bill. But it was located near Delaware Street. If they are referring to a burger restaurant that was nearer to the railroad tracks, which used to be located where Fairfield and Suisun City met before the Highway 12 overpass opened in 1984, then that would be the C.&K. Drive-In. It was built on the old California Packing Company's lot and opened in 1955. A picture of the restaurant in the 1956 Armijo La Mezcla yearbook included that it was open twenty-four hours a day and had the tagline "Where Fairfield and Suisun Meet."

Beverly Mealer: I helped teach the tiny tot classes at the M&M Skating Rink in Suisun. I spent so much time on my skates, I could drive my car with them on. I used to call in orders of hash browns with gravy and ketchup to C.&K. (don't judge, it was delicious), jump in my '54 Chevy with a stick shift and drive down to get them. I'd roll in and roll out, jump back in the car and head back to the rink. Those were the days!

The C.&K. Drive-In was near the Union Avenue city limits of Fairfield and Suisun City decades before the Highway 12 overpass split them. *Armijo High yearbook, 1956.*

MR. STEAK OR HAPPY STEAK?

These two steak places were contemporaries and were both located on North Texas Street and had similar names. So it is not surprising that some old-time Fairfielders have often confused them with one another.

By the time Fairfield got its own Mr. Steak in August 1969, the franchise already had more than three hundred restaurants and was opening a new one every four days. The Fairfield Mr. Steak was located at 2100 North Texas Street, featured seating for 128 patrons, had a used brick front and a shake shingle roof, which gave it a Western look. A three-dimensional molded plastic cartoonish cow's head, the franchise's logo, was placed in the front of the building.

Mr. Steak offered USDA choice corn-fed beef. It was known for its T-bone steak, teriyaki steak, frontier steak, Alaskan king crab, filet steak and more. At lunchtime, its Continental Hamburger, which had ground beef, breadcrumbs, cream of mushroom soup and Swiss cheese, was one of the most popular items on the menu.

Gam's Restaurant, an all-you-can-eat place, opened at 1767 North Texas Street on the corner of Oak Street in 1965. It offered different all-you-can-eat menus daily for $1.50. These menus included roast beef or chicken and dumplings on Sunday, Mexican beef enchiladas on Monday, Salisbury steak on Tuesday, beef burgundy on Wednesday, braised short ribs on Thursday, grilled filet of sole on Friday and barbecue short ribs on Saturday. It offered pan-fried chicken every day.

In 1969, Happy Steak opened in the old Gam's location. Its tagline was "Home of the Golden Spud." A 1971 advertisement reported that "every steak served is cut and processed in our own meat cutting plant by qualified happy meat cutters." Everything in the advertisement was happy. The meat cutters, the smiling golden spud, heck, even a cow that is evidently pleased as punch to make the ultimate sacrifice for the restaurant was beaming.

While its reasonably priced T-bone or sirloin steaks, not to mention its shrimp, lobster, chicken and beef kabobs, were popular, one of the most cited menu items many remember was the cheese toast.

Fairfielders recalled some choice memories of Mr. Steak and Happy Steak:

> *Rick Perez: We went to Mr. Steak a number of times when I was little. Mom and Dad would place the same order for steaks, and Dad always complained that mom got the better cut.*

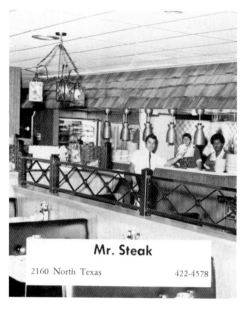

Left: Often confused with Happy Steak, also on North Texas Street, Mr. Steak opened in 1969. *Armijo High yearbook, 1970.*

Right: A 1969 Happy Steak grand opening advertisement. *Fairfield Civic Center Library microfilm.*

Rick Laughlin: I remember Mr. Steak. The steaks were comparable to Sizzler, I guess. But the price was right, and I was poor, so it worked for me.

Sherri Kemper-Joyce: I recall smoke—just clouds of smoke while I was eating!

Anthony Hall: If you took a "steak break at Happy Steak" while Joel Gibson, Tony Hall and Kenny Totman worked there, we apologize for the mayhem which ensued! The same things happened every night—impersonating Elvis Presley over the intercom system to announce orders, chasing each other around the restaurant, throwing plastic lids, whipped cream and baked potatoes, and then there was the time Totman crashed through the glass front door while we were chasing each other and sliding around on the wet floors after mopping.

WHICH DAIRY ARE YOU TALKIN' 'BOUT? DAIRY BELLE, DARI-DELITE OR DAIRY QUEEN?

Dairy Belle had its grand opening on November 18, 1961, at 1615 West Texas Street in the building that was later the home of Sno-White No. 2, You's Burgers and the Jelly Donut. The location was just 236 feet away from the Hi-Fi Drive-In and its twenty-four-cent Steakburgers, so to compete on opening day, Dairy Belle sold its burgers for a mere ten cents. It also served milkshakes, double-decker quarter-pound burgers, chili dogs, white fish sandwiches, banana splits and more.

The original owners were Glen and Margaret Robaugh, who sold it two years later to Glen and Ollie Gorrell.

Then in March 1964, just two and a half miles down the road at the odd-shaped building located at 2260 North Texas Street, Dari-Delite Drive-In opened its doors for the first time. The primary source record is a little confusing, because an announcement about the grand opening in February 1964 lists old Dairy Belle owner Glen Robaugh as the owner of the new place. But then the grand-opening announcement in March lists Jim and Marge Edman as the owners.

To further muddy the waters, eventually, the owner who most old-timers remember was Emily Swetland—who, by the way, had worked at Dairy Belle.

OPENING SALE
Sat., Nov. 18
Bring the Whole Famliy

DAIRY BELLE
BURGERS 10¢

DAIRY BELLE THICK
SHAKES 19¢ CHOC. VANILLA STRAW. EA

DAIRY BELLE
DRIVE-IN
1615 W. Texas   Fairfield
Open: 10:30 a.m. to 10 p.m.   Owned and Operated by Glenn & Margerie Robaugh

A 1961 Dairy Belle grand opening advertisement. *Fairfield Civic Center Library microfilm.*

Since Texas is the Dairy Queen capital of the world, with close to six hundred restaurants in the Lone Star State, it is wholly fitting that Fairfield's lone DQ was located on West Texas Street—at 1730 West Texas Street to be exact.

Now, Vacaville has East Monte Vista, which many call Hamburger Hill due to the plethora of fast food outlets, but there's no clever name for the burger joints and other eateries on West Texas Street that included Dairy Queen, Hi-Fi Drive-In, Dairy Belle, Smorga Bob's, Johanne's Hot Dogs and others, but perhaps there should be.

So, to review, Fairfield had a Dairy Belle, Dari-Delite and Dairy Queen—oh, and Holland Dairy, but that was a completely different kind of thing.

Dari-Delite opened in the oddly shaped building that later became Crunchy's, Eucalyptus Records and Tapes, a vacuum store and more. *Armijo High yearbook, 1967.*

Locals shared their dairy and dari memories:

Gail Kneezle-Reed: Dari-Delite was my very first job in 1966, when I was a junior at Armijo High School. I made $1.35 per hour. They had fries, tacos and some type of deep-fried Hawaiian thing that I think were called Hawaiian Konas. For twenty-five cents, you could buy this enormous cone filled with either vanilla or chocolate frosty ice cream. I used to fill my friends' cones so high, it was a balancing act! I would also make gigantic hamburgers for them. I was only sixteen and didn't realize I wasn't supposed to super-size everything for my friends!

Johnnie Laird: I could eat five Dari-Delite burgers no problem. Actually, five of those probably wouldn't equal one Dave's Burger.

Gina Kramm: One of the biggest impressions on me when I worked at Dairy Queen were the darling senior couples who were regulars. They had been going out for ice cream every Friday night since they'd started dating way back when. It made me sigh and think, "I want a love like that!"

COLONIAL KITCHEN OR COLONY KITCHEN?

According to a July 1958 newspaper announcement, the Colonial Kitchen opened at 431 Union Avenue in a bright-red building. Many locals recall it as being pink, but it may have faded. The building was used as the Lions Club's headquarters. In any event, the restaurant was originally run by the Merrell family, who moved to Fairfield from Ventura. The Colonial Kitchen specialized in home-cooked food, homemade breads and pie. It also served southern fried chicken, baked Virginia ham, ambrosia salad, candied yams, broccoli in lemon butter and other delights.

A 1959 advertisement stated that it was "The Restaurant Where You'll Send Your Friends." It listed, evidently as selling points, the fact that it had neither a bar nor a jukebox, which may have been a not-too-subtle code for "no drunks" and "no teenagers hanging out."

Now, the similarly named Colony Kitchen didn't open until thirteen years later, on June 10, 1971. It was a family diner located at 2980 Travis Boulevard. The two restaurants coexisted for about thirteen years.

In December 1983, Denny's operated more than one thousand restaurants in the United States and more than two hundred abroad. The next year, it acquired seventy-eight Colony Kitchen restaurants for a price of $11.3 million. By 1985, the Fairfield Colony Kitchen had become Denny's No. 2 and oddly was a hop, skip and a jump away from Denny's No. 1 at 1360 Holiday Lane.

By the way, evidently just to add to the Colonial Kitchen and Colony Kitchen confusion, Colonial Lady Fried Chicken opened in Vacaville in 1980.

A Colony Kitchen advertisement from 1971. *Fairfield Civic Center Library microfilm.*

SPEAKING OF COLONY KITCHEN:
DID IT BECOME VICKI'S DRIVE-IN?

Nope. They were contemporaries. As stated previously, Colony Kitchen's address was 2980 Travis Boulevard, and Vicki's Drive-In was behind it at 1740 Holiday Lane.

DID LONG JOHN SILVER'S BECOME SKIPPER'S
OR VICE-VERSA?

The short answer is no.

These two fried fish restaurants were only four hundred feet apart. Long John Silver's Seafood Shoppe at 2263 North Texas Street opened in 1976, and Skipper's Seafood and Chowder House, at 2285 North Texas, came along two years later. It is not surprising that they are confused with each other or that folks think one replaced the other.

Skipper's closed years ago, and while there is technically still a Long John Silver's in Fairfield, it is combined with KFC and is no longer at the same location.

Locals recall deep-fried memories of both fish joints:

Cliff Jackson: My dad called Long John Silver's Short Jack Gold's. We still get it occasionally here in Dallas. I went at least once a week in college for the giant platter with two or three filets, six shrimp, French fries, hushpuppies, clams and a bunch of those wonderful little crispies. That's probably what happened to my gallbladder. It's terrible for you but oh so good!

Alice Jones: David's English Fish and Chips was soooo much better. Real cod.

Kelvin Wade: I remember going to Skipper's often with my friend Chumly. We'd hang out there, smoking cigars and drinking beer. It's weird to think you could ever smoke in restaurants.

Kitty Coleman: I loved our manager at Skipper's, Kathleen Mahoney! I miss her so much and wish I could give her a hug! The stories I have with her at Skippers are priceless. When I won employee of the year, I ended up on the wrong airplane. I was supposed to fly to Tacoma, Washington, but went to Ontario, Canada. I called Kathleen and told her I was so sorry and thought I was in so much trouble. She told me to hold on because she was laughing too hard. Then I started laughing. She taught me to laugh and learn!

Nicole Hanson: My parents took me to lunch during Skipper's grand opening, and I started choking. The manager started to freak out thinking it was on a bone—it was just their awesome spaceship-shaped ice! I got some free ice cream!

WHICH JUANITA?

Have you ever had that little niggling voice in the back of your mind telling you that something just ain't right?

I had that whenever I heard Fairfielders talk about a woman named Juanita who owned a restaurant in Fairfield on North Texas Street. According to my research, that would have been Juanita Musso, who owned swanky upscale eatery Voici (see chapter 3, "Unique, Classy, Feedbag: The Fairfield Sit-Down Restaurant Spectrum").

Now, most people talked about how nice and classy she was and how her style and elegance was reflected in the establishment she ran. Everything had to be just so—décor, atmosphere and cuisine—the total package.

Then there were other stories that some told about her that just did not jibe with the person others had described or the restaurant.

Longtime local Gene Thacker said Juanita was a large woman of about three hundred pounds who always wore a floral-printed muumuu and went braless. He said she had a penchant for coming up behind male customers and unsuspectingly giving them "flesh earmuffs"—wrapping her enormous muumuu-covered breasts around the sides of their heads.

Fairfield Mayor Gary Falati remembered going to Voici and seeing Juanita walking around with a rooster on her shoulder and asking diners, "Wanna see my cock?"

Also, a few hinted or outright said that she had also been a Bay Area madam years before.

Muumuu? Booby earmuffs? A rooster? In swanky Voici? That just never added up to me.

Then I searched posts in the "I Grew Up in Fairfield, Too" Facebook group for Juanita, and thankfully, Mademoiselle Google, Ancestry.com and the Polk City Directories cleared it all up for me.

So get this, there were *two* Juanitas who owned restaurants on North Texas Street. Juanita Musso ran Voici that was noted for its classy interior and her glitzy handmade Christmas ornaments from 1960 to her death in 1980.

Then there was Juanita Musson, who ran Juanita's Galley in the Fairfield Bowl in the early 1980s.

That's right. Juanita Musso and Juanita Musson.

Now it is quite easy to see how people could confuse them, especially since it was decades ago. I mean, even though they were not Fairfield restauranteurs at the same time, what are the odds you would have two women in the same business on the same street in the same city with names

Idiosyncratic restauranteur Juanita Musson at her restaurant in the Fairfield Bowl in 1982. *Public domain.*

that are so similar? Well, come to think of it, the odds are probably the same as having two Denny's within walking distance of each other and having a Colony Kitchen and Colonial Kitchen as contemporaries as well.

Evidently, the similarities in their names and their professions are pretty much where any resemblance ends with the two Juanitas.

There is very little about Voici's Juanita Musso on the internet, but if you search for informaion on Juanita Musson, fasten your seatbelt and be prepared to go down a very long, wild, fascinating and unique rabbit hole.

Musson opened and closed at least eleven restaurants from the 1950s to the 1980s and is best known for operating Juanita's Galley in Sausalito, which was located in the decommissioned paddlewheel ferry the *Charles Van Damme* that was beached on the mudflats there.

Musson was an incredible cook who had absolutely no filter. What she thought she said and what she said was often profane and directed at customers. According to the 2005 Arcadia Publishing book *Images of America: Sausalito*:

- Juanita Musson was an avid animal lover and allowed wild and domesticated beasts, including an orphaned deer, a white pig named Erica and a woolly monkey named Beauregard as well as roosters, cats, dogs and goats to wander freely about her establishments.
- If she was upset with a patron, she might throw a rolling pin or a skillet at them or dump their plate of food into their lap. One of her catchphrases was, "Eat it, or wear it!"
- Customers were required to pour their own coffee and to write out their food selections on order pads that had printed on them: "Our food guaranteed—but not the disposition of the cook." Diners could check a box and choose the level of service they desired: Slow, Don't Care, or Damn Big Rush. However, after the boxes, it said, "Doesn't mean that you still get what you ask for—but check any one that will make you feel better."

Legendary *San Francisco Chronicle* columnist Herb Caen described the richness of the food Juanita Musson served in his inimitable way. Caen said she was "the West Coast distributor of cholesterol" and that "the American Medical Association has put her on its most wanted list."

Many of the idiosyncrasies that Musson exhibited in her Sausalito spot, as well as others in the Bay Area, were also present when she ran the Juanita's Galley in the Fairfield Bowl. The difference was that Musson's wackiness was well-documented by then, and the Fairfield environmental health inspectors weren't having any of it. They cracked down on her until the only animals in the restaurant were the nameless ones on the menu.

By the way, the rooster that Gary Falati had seen on her (not Juanita Musso's) shoulder was named Sombitch, and he replaced an earlier crowing bird named Chickenshit.

One last thing I want to set straight is that Juanita Musson (and Juanita Musso, by those confusing the two) was said by some to have been a madam in the past. That is not true and is probably due to Musson being confused with Sally Stanford, a Sausalito restauranteur who was a contemporary of Musson's in the 1950s (they were "frenemies"). Stanford *had* been a madam and later became the Sausalito mayor.

So how big a personality was Juanita Musson? Well, to try to capture just a smidgen of her vivaciousness, author Sally Hayton-Keeva needed to write not one but two books about her: *The Eat It or Wear It Cookbook* and *Juanita! The Madcap Adventures of a Legendary Restaurateur.*

A painting of Juanita Musson with a rolling pin by artist Heidi Snowden. *Courtesy of Heidi Snowden.*

Juanita Musson died in 2011 at the age of eighty-seven.

Locals shared colorful memories of Juanita Musson (not Musso):

> *Garrett Smith: If you said you didn't like your food, she would come out and bring the monkey and a skillet.*

> *Brian Evan Sweet: That monkey named Beauregard used to steal your drinks.*

> *Nancy Glashoff Tiedeman: Yeah, she was something else. Our family went to dinner when she was at the bowling alley, and she really embarrassed my dad by getting behind him and kind of wrapping her breasts around him. Can you imagine—MY DAD?*

DID POLITICAL CORRECTNESS CAUSE NEARLY ALL OF THE SAMBO'S RESTAURANTS, INCLUDING FAIRFIELD'S, TO CLOSE?

From time to time, someone will post a picture of a Sambo's Restaurant in a nostalgia-themed Facebook group. Members will then post memories of Sambo's pancakes or coffee, and then, invariably, someone will post something along the lines of: "Too bad they all got shut down except one because of political correctness."

The staying power of a false narrative comes from the fact that it's sometimes easier to believe and perpetuate something that fits into your particular worldview rather than put in the hard work to seek out the truth. In this case, however, the false narrative breaks down with a simple search on Google.

The "political correctness shut down all the Sambo's" false narrative reminds me of the "gold-digging woman sues McDonald's for spilling her own coffee and gets $3 million" story. The award-winning documentary *Hot Coffee* details what actually happened: The woman had third-degree burns on 16 percent of her body, including her thighs and genitals. McDonald's coffee was served at 180-190° Fahrenheit (30 to 40 degrees hotter than competitors), and they had known about the problem for ten years, as there were seven hundred other cases of adults and children being burned.

So back to Sambo's. Here's a little history: the first Sambo's restaurant opened in 1957 in Santa Barbara and was founded by Sam Battistone and F. Newell Bohnett, who combined their names to make Sambo. The chain's seventy-third franchise opened in Fairfield in 1968. It could have been included in the "Reincarnated Restaurants" chapter, as it was later Season's, Baker's Square, Pacific Rice Kitchen, the Fire Pit, La Cabaña de Fairfield, Sandy's 101 Omelettes and, in 2022, Hot Stone Korean Kitchen.

Soon after its founding, Sambo's adapted concepts from an 1899 children's book by Helen Bannerman called *The Story of Little Black Sambo*. It's about an Indian boy who loses his clothing to tigers who then chase each other around a tree, and inexplicably, the tigers melt into butter, which Sambo then puts on pancakes and eats.

The term *sambo* is a pejorative term for Black Americans, which dates back to at least the Civil War era. While the images Sambo's Restaurants used were of a light-skinned Indian boy, nonetheless, the name itself carried divisive connotations of the worst stereotypes of Black people.

The Fairfield Sambo's, which did not close due to political correctness but rather fiscal mismanagement on an epic scale. *Tim Farmer collection.*

Municipalities and other organizations, including the NAACP, protested the chain's name in court cases as early as 1971. But did those protests somehow suddenly make a company that, at its peak, had more than 1,100 restaurants in forty-seven states close all but the original one?

How?

If that had actually happened, it would be one of the most obvious examples of people-powered protests. Shouldn't there be an easy-to-find detailed record of how exactly that went down in books or videos or somewhere on the internet?

There isn't, because that ain't what happened.

To be sure, the protests against Sambo's' name were real and did affect the brand, but that was basically a public relations problem. Sambo's' real—and ultimately fatal—issues were financial. What led directly to the closures of all but one restaurant was a (mis)management plan that destroyed their bottom line called "fraction-of-the-action."

The following is from a November 27, 1981 article in the *New York Times* called "Market Place; Mistakes at Sambo's":

The company's problems hark back to the mid-1970s and relate to Sambo's "fraction-of-the-action" manager-partnership program, an incentive- and capital-generating idea largely responsible for Sambo's early success.

Under the program, managers were entitled to 20 percent of the profits of their stores. Managers could also buy up to another 30 percent interest in 5 percent increments. Sambo's supervisory employees also had "fraction-of-the-action" options. Proceeds from the "action units" were included in the income statement, and this became critically important to Sambo's bottom line. But as the chain expanded, it became increasingly difficult to add stores at an ever faster rate so that earnings from these participants would continue to rise.

The Securities and Exchange Commission investigated the Sambo's plan in 1977 and basically concluded it was a pyramid scheme. Sambo's immediately discontinued the practice, which led to heavy losses. The company earned $22.8 million in 1977. After dumping "fraction-of-the-action" in 1978, the company made $7.6 million. Sambo's then lost $50 million in 1979.

Managers who'd profited handsomely from the scheme sued, and eventually, seven hundred—70 percent—of them resigned. The dominoes began to fall. Rebranding attempts failed, and in 1981, the company filed for bankruptcy. By 1982, only the original Sambo's in Santa Barbara was left.

There are numerous other articles online and at least two books on why Sambo's actually folded. Fighting a PR battle didn't help, but the company's own market mistakes are what doomed it.

The following is one final example:

Two boxers square off. The first boxer has an offensive name on his trunks. The second boxer takes offense and protests. The first boxer then lands thundering haymakers, painful uppercuts and crushing body blows...*to himself* until he is knocked out. The second boxer might be satisfied, but his protest over the offensive trunks wasn't the direct cause of the knockout.

That's what happened to Sambo's.

INTERLUDE: MISSION IMPOSSIBLE CONCLUSION, NO WIENERSCHNITZEL IN FAIRFIELD BACK IN THE DAY

As I picked up the box on my porch delivered by Amazon moments earlier, I heard the now-familiar sounds of a fuse burning and Lalo Schifrin's dramatic staccato *Mission Impossible* theme playing.

I opened the box, and inside was an envelope and a Lloyds Miniature Recorder. I opened the envelope, revealing a picture of Andy's Pawn Shop on North Texas Street, then pressed play on the recorder.

> *Good morning, Mr. Wade. A question was asked by a member of the "I Grew Up in Fairfield, Too" Facebook group: Was there ever a Wienerschnitzel (the fast-food restaurant that specializes in hot dogs) in Fairfield back in the day? Your fellow secret agents of the Impossible Missions Force (IMF) are busy doing covert missions against dictators, evil organizations and crime lords. You, however, are best suited to handle this particular case, as it involves trivia that no one outside the Fairfield city limits (and many inside) care about in the least. Your mission, Tony, should you decide to accept it, is to uncover the truth here. This tape will self-destruct in five seconds.*

As the tape started to smolder, I knew I was up to the mission and accepted it. After all, hadn't I successfully solved the great "Why are Two Fairfield Denny's so Close to Each Other" mystery and the "Did the FART Bus Become the DART Bus" conundrum?

After reading the comments in the Facebook group, I knew I needed to address something else first: this persnickety thing we call memory.

I learned years ago never to trust memories—including my own—when I asked when the old Armijo Auditorium was torn down. The answers I got, which people swore were correct, ranged from 1964 to 1990. Yet no one had the correct date: October 12, 1985.

There is plenty of research on false memories or memory construction in which the subconscious fills in memory gaps. The following is from a 2015 study titled "Memory Gaps and Memory Errors":

> *Memory is a reconstructive process, relying on preexisting shared knowledge to help us comprehend and interpret what we experience. A reliance on prior knowledge is a vital aid to communication and comprehension but, as a consequence, results in the modification of some details in an event, the addition of other details or even the fabrication of entire new events.*

To illustrate this, I'll use the example of Fairfield High graduate/horror filmmaker Kevin S. Tenney. If Kevin is shooting a scene for a movie, at the end of the day, he has what, in the business, are called dailies—raw, unedited footage. Later, he edits the film into a finished product that makes sense and tells the story he wants to tell.

Recalling memories is sometimes more like reviewing an edited film rather than raw footage, and critically, the one reviewing it can't tell the difference.

So on to the mission. All roads in this case lead to Andy's Pawn Shop. That's where some say the Wienerschnitzel was before the pawn shop was there. According to my research, that could not be the case.

I've communicated with the owners, and they said, as it says on the building, that Andy's was founded in 1958 and that it has always been in that location. Some have suggested that at one point it was located downtown, but that was a different pawn shop. The earliest relevant Polk City Directory at the Fairfield Civic Center Library is from 1961, and it lists under "Pawnbrokers" Andy's Military Supply and Loan at 2301 North Texas Street, Fairfield Loan Office at 1025 Texas Street (most likely the one some have confused with Andy's) and Texas Loan and Jewelry Co. at 1562 North Texas Street.

Andy's Military Supply and Loan (later Andy's Pawn Shop) was in the same location it is in now. Yes, the address is now 2385, but that is because the street numbers changed in 1969. This has happened in other parts of Fairfield as well.

Tony Wade didn't use one of those cool old-school spy cameras when doing his Wienerschnitzel research but wishes he had. *From Pixabay.*

There definitely was not a Wienerschnitzel at that location.

Here's why: Wienerschnitzel was founded in 1961 in Southern California. Andy's was in that spot at least as early as 1960, as the 1961 Polk City Directory is for the previous year.

The most common memory mistake many have made is confusing the old Fairfield hot dog joint Johanne's with Wienerschnitzel. Johanne's, which held its grand opening on August 1, 1970, was located at 1708 West Texas Street, across from West Texas Street (later Allan Witt) Park.

Some have even suggested that Johanne's was a Wienerschnitzel beforehand. Just stop it. I have two write-ups from back then—one from the grand opening and the other a 1970 year-end edition of the *Daily Republic*—and one would assume they would have included such information as it being an old Wienerschnitzel spot, but there's nothing like that. It was a new building.

The Dairy Queen that used to be on West Texas Street also sold hot dogs, and some conflate that as well.

The conclusion? Restaurants generally want the community to know they are open for business, and most advertise. Some support the community by, say, sponsoring Little League teams, or at the very least, they are listed in city directories. I've heard from zero Fairfielders who ever played on a

Wienerschnitzel-sponsored sports team, and between the years 1961 and 1991, in the Polk City Directories at the library, Wienerschnitzel is never listed. I have also never seen advertisements in microfilm or in vintage Armijo and Fairfield High yearbooks.

Now perhaps there was a secret local Wienerschnitzel that operated like a speakeasy during Prohibition, but barring that, I can say with high confidence that aside from the newer Wienerschnitzel located in what was a Jack in the Box restaurant out in Cordelia, there has never been a Wienerschnitzel in Fairfield.

That high confidence was heightened when I recently discovered an advertisement for Frank's Drive-In from 1968. It was located at 2365 North Texas Street and owned and operated by Frank Schinka, the former chef manager of the Apache Dining Room and Ernie's Steak House, both located in the Fairfield Bowl. The advertisement says it was in the spot where a short-lived hot dog joint named Super Dog used to be, and checking the address in Polk City Directories, it was *right next door* to Andy's Pawn Shop. So, that's why some misremembered a hot dog place where Andy's is located.

Case closed.

Now, just to be completely clear, wiener schnitzel, thin pieces of veal fillet covered in breadcrumbs and fried in a lot of butter, *was* served in Fairfield. It was available at the Airline Café when it was run by the Dudleys and offered authentic German dishes. But a Wienerschnitzel restaurant in Fairfield? Nein.

8

Some Suisun City Spots

There are people with otherwise chaotic and disorganized lives, a certain type of person that's always found a home in the restaurant business in much the same way that a lot of people find a home in the military.
—American chef Anthony Bourdain

With this chapter, I'm giving a little love—and space in a book that is really about Fairfield—to our unofficial sister city across the tracks. Aside from the four eateries highlighted in this chapter, there were scores of others that Suisunites and Fairfielders frequented, including but not limited to, the Limit, Josiah Wings, Country Kitchen, Puerto Vallarta, Harbor Lights, Tasuke, the Top Notch Café, the Soul Kitchen, First National Bank Bar and Café and many others.

THE MINT: FROM CANDY TO COCKTAILS
TO COMIC BOOKS

With the exception of just a couple of years, there has been some sort of business located at 609 Main Street in Suisun City since approximately 1906. For the purposes of this book, the story of the Mint Grill (also known as the Mint Café, Jimmie's Place and Miss Bea's Mint) began with Yozo Ikenaga and his candy and ice cream shop, which he expanded into a restaurant, as discussed in chapter 1.

A commissioned painting of the downtown Suisun City of yesteryear by artist Donna Covey, which includes Jimmie's Mint Café and H-Jay's. *Donna Covey Paintings.*

Yozo Ikenaga closed the Mint Grill down in 1940 to move his operations to his new venture, the Park Inn (later the site of the Black Swan and the Ranch House), with his daughter and brother. From the mid-1940s until today, it has been owned by the Ciambetti/Harter family.

Giacinto Giampetti was born in 1895 in Abruzzo, Italy, and came to the United States in 1913. He Americanized his name somewhat, as was popular at the time, to James Ciambetti and went by Jimmie. In 1946, he married Berscelia Logan, affectionately called Bea, who was born in 1905 in Byrdstown, Tennessee.

That same year, they took over the Mint Café. At that time, it was a restaurant and later became a restaurant and bar with a separate entrance for each.

While the extent of Jimmie and Bea's formal education didn't go past grade school, they evidently knew a thing or two about business, as they ran the Mint for decades.

170

James "Jimmie" Ciambetti and Berscelia "Miss Bea" Ciambetti, who owned the Mint Café. *Courtesy of Michelle Marquardt.*

The interior of the Mint Café. *Courtesy of Michelle Marquardt.*

One of the things they added to the building was a staircase and a room in the second level, where they could look down on the patrons participating in illegal gambling in the back room.

Perhaps they needed more eyes on the exterior of the building. In 1947, an article in a Vallejo newspaper described Suisun as "California's Reno" when it came to gambling. Suisun City police chief A.C. Tillman arrested Jimmie and five other operators of local spots for craps and dice games, including proprietors of the Limit, the Target Club and Elmo's. They all paid fines of $300 ($3,750 in 2022).

But that was just the start of the Ciambettis' brushes with the authorities.

In 1955, the Department of Alcoholic Beverage Control of California charged the Ciambettis with two violations. The first was having refilled two one-quart bottles of whiskey against federal regulations. The second and much more serious charge was that, for some time, Bea was not the sole owner of the business as her license purported and that Jimmie was the actual owner. The authorities claimed that this violated several statutes and recommended indefinite suspension of the business's liquor license.

Jimmie plead guilty to the refilling liquor bottles charge, which appears to have been a deal to have the same charge dropped against his wife. He was put on three years' probation.

The Ciambettis fought the second charge tooth and nail, and it took years to finally be resolved. According to a newspaper article in 1957, Bea was also dinged for selling to an intoxicated person while waiting for the previous case to be adjudicated. Interestingly, in the same piece about that incident, Juanita and John Musso, the later owners of Voici restaurant in Fairfield, were penalized for sales to a minor at their Bank Club in Vallejo.

In 1958, Bea won the case on appeal. The bottom line was that no matter whose name was on the checks a business used or even on the club's marquee outside, the person who actually owned the license owned the business. The relevant case, *Ciambetti V. Department of Alcoholic Beverage Control of California*, is still cited as a precedent in the California Alcoholic Beverage Control Act.

Jimmie Ciambetti in front of the Mint Café. *Courtesy of Michelle Marquardt.*

So although the restaurant/bar was not known by the name Miss Bea's Mint until after Jimmie's death in 1968, it technically was always Miss Bea's Mint.

By the early 1960s, the Mint was basically a bar and as such had several colorful regulars with stories like real-life characters on the TV show *Cheers*. The unofficial inside-joke tagline for the Mint was "The Cultural Mecca of Upper Solano County."

Longtime Suisun City residents and siblings Jimmy Harter and Michelle Marquardt, the grandchildren of the Ciambettis, both worked for years in their grandparents' establishment. Along with Jimmy's son John, they relayed a few of the passed-down stories from the Mint:

> *An old gentleman named Budgie was a regular, and he liked to stand in the doorway and did so for approximately twenty-five years whenever he came to the club. Now in the mid-1970s, Max Baer Jr. (who played Jethro Bodine on the TV show The Beverly Hillbillies and was the son of former heavyweight boxing champion Max Baer Sr.) was in town to shoot his movie The McCullochs. He told Budgie to move out of the doorway because he needed to get a shot for the film. Budgie said, "I hope you're a better fighter than your dad was if you think you can tell me what to do!" Bea bribed him with a drink to come sit at the bar.*
>
> *On St. Patrick's Day, many former Suisun City mayors, including Guido Colla, Bill Jones and Manual Baracosa, would cook corned beef outside in the empty lot where Elmo's had been before burning down. A rookie police officer came by one year and told them they couldn't be cooking out there. Guido told him to go back to the station and have his boss come back and tell them that.*
>
> *A neighborhood dog named Rags, who was owned by a guy named Charlie, would daily visit many Suisun businesses on Main Street. At the Mint, he was considered the mascot and had his own little barstool.*

Around 1990, Bea retired due to failing health and a downturn in the business, and she passed away in 2002. From 1991 to 2003, 609 Main Street was the home of Scoundrels Hair Salon. After it folded, John Harter, a victim of the dot-com bubble bursting, decided to follow a long-held dream of opening his own comic book shop. Waterfront Comics debuted in 2003 and is still doing a brisk business in 2022.

John had developed his love of comic books at a young age, and it may be genetic. When his father Jimmy was only about eight years old, he would

Waterfront Comics at 609 Main Street Suisun City, owned by John Harter. His great-grandparents had owned the Mint Café in the same location. *Courtesy of John Harter.*

have a daily task of delivering a double shot of whiskey to the owner of the White Elephant store down the street. The payment for his prepubescent alcohol delivery services? A used comic book.

H-JAYS

The restaurant/bar at 605 Main Street had been known as the Oasis and then H-Jay's. In 1972, Frank and Tessie Rogers became the owners. Running the restaurant/bar was a family affair, as their daughters, Barbara, Toni and Tammy, worked there as well.

New York steak, seafood, prime rib, lobster tails and homemade peach cobbler were popular menu items, as was the clam chowder. Many locals remember H-Jays being the first place where they tried frog legs. Like Voici in Fairfield, it became the go-to spot for movers and shakers.

Suisun City Mayor/Solano County Supervisor Jim Spering: Before we built the overpass that split Fairfield and Suisun, all the judges and members of the board of supervisors went there, and a lot of business got done. I remember when I was mayor and we needed help from the supervisors as we were trying to figure out what to do with the redevelopment and the waterfront, we met with a lot of people at H-Jays.

Toni Todd recalled a funny incident that happened there in the mid-1970s.

Max Baer Jr. came in, and he was wearing an orange jumpsuit and smoking a skinny cigar. He was filming a movie. It was lunchtime, and he wanted to talk to the owner. He said he wanted all the cars moved from the parking lot, and my mom said, "No. Who do you think you are?" I told my mom, "That's Jethro from The Beverly Hillbillies. *He said they wanted to order lunch, so she charged him an arm and a leg.*

H-Jay's was right next door to Miss Bea's Mint, and the respective business owners were friends for years. According to Toni Todd, they would sometimes engage in matchmaking: "Grandma Bea would come over after lunch and joke that they were going to cut a hole in the wall to get me and Jimmy Harter together. That didn't happen."

THE BURRITO PALACE TRAGEDY

The memories of local eateries are so often saturated with joy, but some are mixed with pain and, unfortunately, even tragedy. In the case of the latter, there is perhaps none more tragic locally than the Burrito Palace, which was located at 307 Alder Street in the Marina Center.

Local folks, as well as those who passed by on Highway 12, raved about the Suisun City eatery, especially its super burrito. The food was fresh and authentic.

On October 8, 1988, Pedro Rocha came into the Burrito Palace and ordered two tacos and demanded his wife, Magdalina Rocha-Guitierrez, a waitress there, to sit down with him. She refused because she was on duty. Pedro Rocha became enraged, grabbed an eight-inch knife from the restaurant counter and stabbed his wife several times. Magdalina Rocha-Guitierrez, who was only twenty-nine years old, was pronounced dead on arrival at NorthBay Medical Center later that night.

According to a newspaper account, when police arrived after the stabbing, a crowd of about three hundred people who were there for the annual carnival at the Marina Center had gathered outside the restaurant.

Suisun City's Burrito Palace on the night of the horrific 1988 murder. *Fairfield Civic Center Library microfilm.*

Individuals in the crowd began throwing rocks at the approximately forty-five police officers from Suisun City, Fairfield, Vacaville, Dixon, the Solano County Sheriff's Department and the California Highway Patrol who were needed to control the throng. Many remember that tragic day as being the end of the carnivals there as well.

Memories of the Burrito Palace are bittersweet, as some recall a nice atmosphere and exquisite food that was forever marred by the unspeakable actions of one man. Eventually, the restaurant relocated to Vacaville and is now run by different owners.

DYNASTY RESTAURANT: SIMPLY THE BEST

Scores of Solano County residents were very sad in 2016, when Dynasty Chinese Restaurant in Suisun City closed, as owners Jimmy and Grace Hung retired. You know who wasn't sad? Other Chinese restaurants.

For over twenty years, the Hungs' Suisun City restaurant, which was located in the Heritage Park Shopping Center on Sunset Avenue, as well as one in Fairfield on Waterman Drive, owned by Jimmy's brother-in-law, Ping Liu, had a stranglehold on the "Best Chinese Restaurant" category in the annual *Daily Republic* Best of Solano Awards.

They were quite literally running out of wall space to hang the framed award plaques each year.

Jimmy was born Kwen Hu Hung in Taiwan in 1951 and came to America in 1982. He was a welder in Collinsville for a year and then began working at the Golden Kirin restaurant in Vallejo as a waiter, a cook and then a manager.

The first restaurant the Hungs owned was the Golden Grill Mongolian Barbecue in 1985 in Suisun City's Sunset Center Shopping Center. Four years later, they opened the Dynasty restaurant across the street, and Ping Liu opened the Fairfield location in 1993.

The atmosphere of Dynasty Suisun City was relaxing and friendly. Patrons recall the gently babbling fishpond near the entrance, the exquisite artwork on the wall and the attentiveness of the wait staff. But of course, the food was the main attraction. Patrons loved the tangy, tart and spicy sauced dishes and the mouth-watering aromas of peanut oil, garlic and scallions wafting in from the kitchen.

NOW OPEN
現代 **Dynasty Restaurant**
MANDARIN CUISINE

1. Jimmy Hung 2. Ping Liu 3. Sue Corduck 4. Hsueh-Mei Hung

Serving Beer and Wine
Lunch & Dinner

Open Seven Days • Mon-Fri 11am-9pm • Sat & Sun 12-9pm
FOOD TO GO 426-6222
254-B Sunset Avenue Suisun City

A Dynasty Restaurant Suisun City advertisement from 1990. *Fairfield Civic Center Library microfilm.*

The menu featured a variety of Chinese cuisines: Mandarin, Szechwan and Cantonese. According to Hung, some of the most popular menu items included Heavenly Chicken (diced breaded chicken, deep-fried with mushrooms and sautéed with teriyaki sauce), Garlic Scallops Hot Pot (scallops with garlic, mushrooms, celery and carrots in brown sauce) and Dynasty Chicken (diced breaded chicken, deep-fried with garlic and ginger in brown sauce).

Jimmy Hung attributed Dynasty's success and esteem in the community to a combination of things, including a good staff, fresh produce and being polite to the customers. The loyalty and love that the Hungs were shown year after year by repeat customers is one of the many things they miss in their well-earned retirement.

"Ninety percent of our customers were regulars who we are thankful for and whom we depended on," Hung said. "We even had customers who moved to Indiana, but every time they came back to the Bay Area, they'd visit us."

Locals recalled sweet and not so sour memories of Dynasty:

Joella Benkelman: This was my father's favorite place. When he died, I ordered the family a meal after the funeral. They were so kind and caring to us.

Brent Finger: Jimmy did the same for my father when he passed away. Jimmy was and still is like family to everyone in my family.

Vanessa Walling-Sisi: They were the best! And the dozens of "Best of Solano" plaques on the wall showed we weren't the only family who thought so. Miss them.

9

Pastries and Desserts

*Dessert is probably the most important stage of the meal, since it will be the last
thing your guests remember before they pass out all over the table.*
—American actor William Powell

I think it's fair to say that Fairfielders, from the days of stagecoaches all the way to hands-free Teslas, have always had a serious sweet tooth. There have been far too many local shops dedicated to sweet treats to delve deeply into all of them, but a few are spotlighted in this chapter. Among the delicacies not covered but definitely remembered are the ginormous banana splits at Leatherby's Family Creamery, the racy and tasty "adult" cakes at Keith's Bakery, the moist poppy seed muffins at Rosanna's, the creamy strawberry smoothies at TCBY (The Country's Best Yogurt) and the lil' chunk of heaven Chocolate Chip Cookies at Mrs. Field's Cookies.

FLAKY CREAM DO-NUTS

Flaky Cream Do-Nuts opened at 726 Texas Street in 1959 with free coffee, do-nuts and free ice cream. The coproprietors were Bill Wills and Carry Marques. It opened in the renovated First National Bank building and featured a self-service coffee bar. In addition to do-nuts, it also served ice cream, hamburgers and steak sandwiches.

Above: A 1985 advertisement for Leatherby's Family Creamery, which used to be on Oliver Road. *Fairfield Civic Center Library microfilm.*

Right: The exterior of Flaky Cream Do-Nuts. *Armijo High yearbook, 1971.*

Locals shared powdered sugar memories:

Paul Shelley: In the '70s, I would go over for breakfast, and the owner would set up a TV and watch old westerns with me.

Ted Williams: I actually met Linda Ronstadt there on a Friday night. She was in town to see her grandmother in 1969.

Mark Weber: I worked there as a janitor, cleaning the offices above Flaky Cream in '77 and '78. I made minimum wage and all of the donuts I could eat!

Julie Huffenberger: I skipped school one day. My friends and I were at Flaky's. I knew an English paper was due, so I wrote it there. It was a very detailed story about…skipping school at Flaky's. I turned it in, and my English teacher Mr. Hahn was so impressed with it, he submitted it to a magazine, and they printed it.

WINCHELL'S DONUT HOUSE

Winchell's Donuts was founded by Verne Winchell on October 8, 1948, in Temple City, California. Winchell soon earned the nickname "The Donut King" as the shops multiplied. Later, the company merged with Denny's Incorporated, and Verne Winchell served as Denny's chairman of the board, president and chief executive officer.

The first Fairfield Winchell's opened on April 3, 1959, near the main gate of Travis Air Force Base on what is now Parker Road. The grand-opening special was a dozen donuts for forty-nine cents. The location that most Fairfielders probably recall opened in 1971 and was located at 760 North Texas Street (in 2022, it is the Lucky Jelly Donut) across from Armijo's athletic fields. Apple fritters, bear claws, brownies, maple bars and fruit punch were offered near Fairfield High as well when the third local shop opened in the Mission Village Shopping Center.

One Fairfielder who was definitely not happy when the first North Texas Street Winchell's set up shop was Dave's Giant Hamburgers owner Dave Heim. Heim had started selling Spudnuts, doughnuts created from potato-based flour, the year before. When Winchell's opened less than half a mile

Left: The grand opening advertisement for the Winchell's near Travis Air Force Base in 1959. *Fairfield Civic Center Library microfilm.*

Right: Winchell's Donuts across the street from Armijo. When it opened, Dave's Giant Hamburgers stopped selling Spudnuts. *Armijo High yearbook, 1979.*

from his burger joint, Heim saw the writing on the wall and quickly got out of the Spudnut business.

Sweet memories from some locals:

> *Vicky McLaurin: I grew up on Winchell's. I blame them for my poor dietary habits.*

> *Holly O'Brien: That's how my family got me to go to church. We got chocolate bars after.*

> *Kathi Sweet: My little sister worked there. We ate her mistakes.*

> *Tony Wade: In high school at Armijo, this guy would bring his older brother's vodka to school in a sealed container then go to Winchell's at lunchtime and buy some orange juice. The guy would mix himself a screwdriver and then drink it in his sixth period school newspaper class. OK, that guy was me.*

Tom McDowell: I cut class at Armijo to go to the Winchell's across the street. Then I worked at the one at Mission Village, became assistant manager at the one across from Armijo, then manager at this one outside of the Travis main gate!

JOHNSON'S PASTRIES AND CAFETERIA

When locals recall now-long-gone Johnson's Pastries and Cafeteria, owned by Gene and Marianne Johnson, they remember the bright-orange booths and the meticulous attention to making sure it was clean, and of course, they delight in memories of the delicacies served.

These menu items included an assortment of pies ranging from peach to lemon meringue, dinner rolls of various types, all kinds of breads, blueberry and raisin bran muffins and much more. But by far the most remembered item from Johnson's was its (sound the regal horns) champagne cake.

All of the Johnsons' children, Judy, Kirk, Kerry and Jennifer, worked at the bakery over its multi-decade run in Fairfield and to this day are always asked about the most famous confection. "We do not have the recipe for my dad's champagne cake. Several people have come forward on Facebook saying they have it, but it is not the right recipe," Judy Johnson said. "It was a chiffon cake with rum flavored custard in between and was decorated with whipped cream dollops on the top and set off with shaved pink chocolate."

Judy Johnson added two more interesting facts: the champagne cake had zero alcohol, and no one in their family actually liked it. "My brother and I liked the double chocolate fudge cake," she said.

Gene Johnson came from a long line of bakers, and he practiced the family craft when he was in the U.S. Navy, stationed aboard a submarine. Gene and his father, Reverend Joseph Emmanuel Johnson, ran a bakery in Leavenworth, Washington, and when they heard that a lot more money could be made in California, they moved to San Jose. They opened Johnson's Bakery on Winchester Avenue in San Jose down from the Winchester Mystery House and ran it there from 1954 to 1961. On Valentine's Day in 1962, they moved to 811 Texas Street in Fairfield. The building had previously housed the weekly *Solano Republican* newspaper.

Judy Johnson was in awe of her father's work ethic. "My dad would get up at 9:00 p.m. and be at work at 10:00 p.m. and work until midnight. He would call my mom at like 11:00 p.m. or midnight, and they would talk

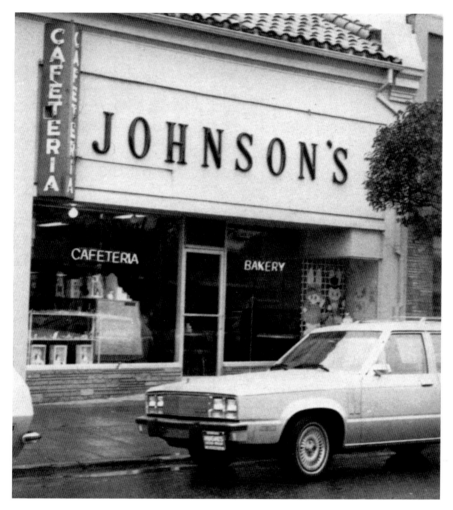

Johnson's Pastries and Cafeteria downtown, the home of—cue the "Hallelujah Chorus"—their famous champagne cakes. *Armijo High yearbook, 1978.*

about business, and then he'd work until 9:00 a.m. He would do that six days a week, and on Sundays, he would go in and make cookies."

Gene Johnson was a stickler for cleanliness. While many bakeries often had the pasty mix of flour and water stuck all over the handles of refrigerators and ovens, he insisted on having surfaces cleaned constantly. "He would say that the bottom of a cake or pie must be clean. When a lady takes a cake and sets it on her nice lace tablecloth and there is a grease stain, she is not going to be happy," Judy Johnson said. "I always remember that when I pick up something at Safeway and it's all greasy on the bottom."

Gene Johnson with a
Johnson's Pastries and
Cafeteria creation.
Courtesy of Judy A. Johnson.

Another Johnson's Bakery memory touchpoint that many locals share was the antique 1931 Ford panel truck Judy's father used for making deliveries. "People would be really upset when he drove very slowly going over railroad tracks, but when he put a sign in the window that said, 'Delivering Another Cake for Johnson's Bakery,' people gave him leeway," Judy Johnson said.

In 1970, Judy was apprenticing with her dad and heard that he had been in a car accident on Sears Point Road. He insisted he was fine and would be at the store at 9:00 p.m., but he had to be taken to the hospital in Vallejo, as he had fainted. It turned out that he had three broken ribs, a punctured lung, a bruised heart and a dislocated shoulder. So Judy called her grandfather to help her, and they got everything done except for one thing: they didn't have the recipe for a champagne cake that was to be picked up the following day. They had to call Gene Johnson at the hospital, and the hospital staff initially told her it was too late to be calling, but she convinced them. She later brought the staff donuts and other pastries for their kindness.

If any locals enjoyed the dinner rolls at Mr. Steak in Fairfield, they can thank Johnson's. They also made rolls for the Flying Tigers on Travis Air Force Base.

While most frequently referred to as Johnson's Bakery, the official name for the establishment was Johnson's Pastries and Cafeteria. As such, it offered much more than just sweet treats. In 1963, customers could get a two-piece fried chicken dinner with vegetables, potatoes, rolls with butter, salad and coffee, and it would only set them back $1.10. A full roast beef dinner with all the trimmings cost only $0.98. In 1983, when it was celebrating its twenty-first anniversary with a mini breakfast featuring one egg, two pieces of bacon or sausage and one piece of toast, it was still only $1.65.

And while this may border on old-school Fairfield blasphemy, there are many Armijo students who gave Johnson's tasty cheeseburgers the nod over Dave's Giant Hamburgers.

The holidays at Johnson's were a predictably busy time. It offered the typical Thanksgiving and Christmas fare—turkey, ham, roast beef and all the delicious side dishes—but also offered a service. Since the establishment had a huge six-shelf oven that cooked evenly, customers could bring in their own meat to be cooked. In addition to the aforementioned ham and turkey, the oven would even cook a whole pig with an apple in its mouth.

The day before Thanksgiving or Christmas, anything left would go to the firehouse to be distributed to needy families.

Gene Johnson died on a golf course in 1981, two days shy of his fifty-fifth birthday. Marianne Johnson remarried in 1983 and kept the restaurant going for a few years before selling it. She died in 1994 at the age of sixty-four.

Locals recalled pink box memories of Johnson's Bakery:

Christina Schauweker: I worked at Johnson's Bakery when I was eighteen. I helped ice cakes and made brownies and cookies. I arrived for work at 5:00 a.m. to the smell of the donuts being made. I was just in a bakery section of a grocery store here in San Diego when I smelled the aroma of donuts, and in my mind, I was right back at Johnson's again forty-plus years later.

Christy Thompson: I loved Johnson's so much! Everything was delicious. As with all the stores and restaurants on Texas Street, one of the things I remember is walking in the back door and through the kitchen. I don't think health codes would be too thrilled about that these days, but it's sure a fun memory.

Janelle Pritchard Hawkins: Mr. Johnson used to come to the dentist I worked for, and he always had an early morning appointment. He always smelled like donuts!

Rebecca Siegfried: My dad worked for the police department, and after World War II, he never wanted to carry a gun again, so he was kind of a Mayberry-style problem solver. He got a call one day to go to Johnson's regarding a man making bizarre gestures. He recognized an old war buddy who hadn't fared so well. The guy had always talked about his love for fishing, and my dad deduced that he was sitting in Johnson's casting out and reeling in with an imaginary pole. He sat down and asked his old friend if he was catching anything. He said, "Naw." Dad suggested he try the spot in his backyard. So his friend picked up his "oars" and rowed out of the bakery. Dad called the VA and asked them to make a welfare check to get his old war buddy some support.

Al Artola Lovett: In addition to the best German chocolate cake ever, my parents always ordered a full uncut brownie sheet for my birthday. The cake was for the obvious gatherings, but I didn't have to share the delectable brownie treasure.

Johnny Colla: I remember smoking in the restaurant because I knew my parents never went there or to Flaky Cream. Hot rosette, coffee and a smoke before school—I thought I was a real grown-up!

BASKIN-ROBBINS

In 1948, American brothers-in-law Burt Baskin and Irv Robbins combined their respective talents as purveyors of ice cream, as well as their last names, to become one of the true giants in the industry. The company is known for its "31 flavors" slogan, which reflects the idea that a customer could have a different ice cream flavor every day of any month.

The first Fairfield Baskin-Robbins was owned and operated by sisters Mary Minakata and Elsie Nakamura from 1969 to 1990.

Elsie and Mary were the offspring of first-generation Japanese immigrants, or Issei. They were Nisei, or second-generation, and were born here. Elsie was born in 1919, and Mary was born in 1921. Thus, they were American citizens. Shortly after Japan bombed Pearl Harbor, the shameful internment of Americans of Japanese descent began. Elsie was sent to the Gila River War Relocation Center near Phoenix, Arizona.

After the war, Elsie married Armijo Class of 1940 graduate Tadashi Nakamura in 1946, and they had three children, James, Steven and Jayne.

Meanwhile, Mary was in Japan, and to get rations, she was forced to vote in an election. As a consequence, the state department revoked her U.S. citizenship. It took ten years to get it back. When she finally did, she came to

Above: Mary Minakata (*left*) and Elsie Nakamura (*right*) the co-owners of Baskin-Robbins. *Courtesy of Jayne Nakamura.*

Opposite: Darin Kermoade worked at the Fairfield Baskin-Robbins in the early 1980s. *Courtesy of Jayne Nakamura.*

San Francisco and worked in a garment factory until she and Elsie decided to go into business together. They opened Fairfield's first Baskin-Robbins on October 4, 1969.

Elsie's daughter Jayne Nakamura recalled how it came to be that they opened the store.

> *Auntie Mary was working in San Francisco at a dress factory. Mom was here in the Suisun Valley, and she and Dad had the ranch, but sometimes,*

it was OK—sometimes, it was rough. She wanted to try something else, and also, she wanted Mary closer because she had promised their mom that she would watch over her. My cousin had a Baskin-Robbins in Napa and heard they were going to open one in Fairfield, and so they applied for it. They had to go for an interview, and the representative said they don't usually do partnerships, but since they were sisters, they were willing to try it out. They went to Vallejo to be trained and opened up the Fairfield store. They didn't have a business background, but they always figured if they tried it, they could do it.

Basically, Mary took care of things inside the store, like the ice cream cake and pie decorating, while Elsie took care of the books and shopping for supplies, like milk and bananas.

Some of the dozens of ice cream flavors featured included Rocky Road, Gold Medal Ribbon, Mint Chocolate Chip, Rainbow Sherbet, Cookies 'n Cream, Peanut Butter and Chocolate, Cherries Jubilee, Daiquiri Ice, Egg Nog, Fudge Brownie and many more. Despite the exotic selection, the biggest seller by far was just plain ol' Vanilla.

Generations of Fairfielders, including the shop's employees, agree that the sweetness of the thirty-one flavors offered was far surpassed by the sweetness of Mary and Elsie.

Marie and Elsie allowed their ice cream scoopers to eat whatever they wanted for free while they were at work. The sisters loved to go to lunch at many local restaurants, including Dan & Ruth's Café, Omodaka and Pelayo's, among others, and would always bring back food for their employees.

> *Jayne Nakamura: They loved to go out to eat, but they would be so tired that when the waitress would come by, the two of them would have their heads down and be fast asleep. The waitress would come back and ask if they were ready to order. They thought they were praying, and it was an awful long prayer!*

Elsie and Mary retired and sold the shop in 1990. In a newspaper article announcement, they thanked the local community for "21derful years."

Elsie died on November 18, 2015, at the age of ninety-six. Mary followed her in death on April 5, 2021, at the ripe old age of one hundred.

Locals shared remembrances:

> *Mike O'Connor: I remember them as an incredibly nice family. Jayne Nakamura worked there, and I played with her brother Jimmy in the band Matrix. They donated products to raffle so we could earn money to buy band equipment! Lots of nice memories stopping by to sample the many flavors.*

> *Erin Hannigan Andrews: I loved these ladies! My dad's real estate office, Hannigan Blue Ribbon Realty, was adjacent to Baskin-Robbins. It was an incentive to visit Dad at work.*

> *Bill Pinkerton: They were the best. After sweltering summer practices for football, we would go there and try to replace the five to ten pounds of water weight we lost.*

> *Debbie Jo Schroeder: Those ladies were so nice and sweet to everybody. I remember I was in Reno and I ran into them, and they were so thrilled that I was from Fairfield and remembered them.*

> *Bill Fischer: Back in the early and mid-'70s, that's where our family would collect prizes from family games and bets from football games. Dad was so cool because everyone was a winner, as we'd all get double scoops.*

Clarissa Correa: I used to go there all the time as a kid. I always loved the ceramic cats they had on the ice cream cake freezer. They told me they were for good luck. Anytime I see one of those cats, it brings back fond memories of that place!

Lisa Garcia Mitchell: They were the most wonderful ladies! I remember going in there in grade school with my best friend, and they would take as payment however much money I had. It was never enough, but it was enough for them.

INTERLUDE: ONE ARM LIKE POPEYE'S, THE OTHER LIKE OLIVE OYL'S

When I worked at Baskin-Robbins in the early 1980s, we had a secret nickname for Elsie and Mary. It was certainly not meant as an insult, but we felt it reflected their diminutive stature and their almost unbearable cuteness. We called them "The Smurfs."

I had worked at the Carl's Jr. down the street, my first job, and working at Baskin-Robbins was a sea change from the stress of fast food. For one thing, most people were in a very good mood when they came into the store. Ice cream tends to have a calming effect on folks. We all scream for ice cream, but we scream with glee, not anger. To be sure, we got the occasional jerk customers, but they were few and very far between.

My friend from church, Albert Warren, put in a good word in for me to get the job, and I worked with John and Jerry Bassler, Paul Brodeur, Darin Kermoade, Kelly Farney, Thomas Basham, Roger Martinez and Elsie's daughter Jayne, among others.

Letting us eat whatever we wanted was great and not so great. I mean, I would work the opening shift sometimes, and my breakfast would be two ginormous scoops of Pralines 'n Cream with strawberry sauce, whipped cream and nuts. When I first started there, I was lanky. Soon, no one was calling me lanky anymore.

Some of the ice cream was incredibly hard, and forming scoops or hand-packing a half gallon container was a serious workout. Unless you were ambidextrous, you ended up with one arm that looked like Popeye's and one that looked like his girlfriend Olive Oyl's.

When I worked at Baskin-Robbins, there was no air conditioning. We had a fan behind the counter, and there were fly fans above each door, but

Public domain images of Popeye the Sailor Man and his girlfriend, Olive Oyl. *From Pixabay*.

they were pointed at the entrance, not at us scoopers. Flies still got in and sometimes they fell into the ice cream. We had to scoop them out before someone got a sugar cone with Chocolate Mousse plus some unwanted extra protein.

The word that comes up time and again when people look back on Elsie and Mary is *nice*. In reference to them, that word should always be in caps and underlined with an exclamation point at the end. I remember once dropping a coin, maybe a nickel or a dime. It rolled under the counter and Mary, then in her sixties, instantly got down on her hands and knees and fished it out for me.

There was a man in his eighties named Owen who would come by every morning and buy a hand-packed pint of Jamoca Almond Fudge. They charged him one dollar, even though it cost at least twice that much back then.

Every couple of months, we would remove the ice cream tubs and completely defrost and clean the freezers. It was a big job that took several hours. Mary would go to Shakey's Pizza Parlor and buy us pizza, chicken and those wondrous Mojo Potatoes for fuel.

We were allowed to listen to music when we worked and I brought a cassette tape of a Swedish virtuoso rock guitarist named Yngwie Malmsteen that at that time was only available as a Japanese import. Mary happily translated the liner notes for me and every time she pronounced his unusual name, it made me giggle.

Every year starting in November, Mary and Elsie would tape a lid onto a pint container, cut a hole in it and stuff dollars into it from time to time for weeks. They would take all the employees out to eat at Fairfield Landing right before Christmas and draw names to see who would win the money.

In 2013, I wrote a "Back in the Day" column about my former bosses called "Baskin-Robbins' Elsie and Mary: Sweeter Than a Sugar Cone." At that time, Elsie had had a stroke, but Mary was just the same as she had been. I was able to tell them how much I loved and appreciated them and that they were the best bosses I ever had. I also shared how many people in the "I Grew Up in Fairfield, Too" Facebook group loved them as well.

Now and then, I think back on those times with Elsie and Mary and treat myself to a double scoop of delicious memories working for two wonderful human beings.

Epilogue

An After-Dinner Mint and a Chef's Kiss

I don't like it when I go to a restaurant and I'm lectured from the menu.
—French chef Eric Ripert

I know some folks enjoy going to a restaurant and having a very animated and super-chatty server. I ain't one of those people. Now, bear in mind, I'm not talking about going someplace where you are a regular and are well-known among the wait staff and vice versa.

I hope I don't sound like a jerk, but I really don't want to know what dish the server prefers, because we are completely different people and have different tastes. I also really don't want a server horning in on my table conversations with people I've come to dine with. I certainly don't mind them having a sense of humor and adding a bit of their own flavor to the rote utterances they have to recite to dozens of customers every day. In fact, I welcome that. I just don't want them to feel like they can whip off their apron and sit down at the table with me like we are old chums or something. No, they are there to perform a specific service, and I am there to enjoy myself and tip them generously.

I say all of this because while writing this book one thing I wanted to avoid was becoming that kind of server. I also didn't want to be the chef/writer that added way too many tablespoons (or cups) of me throughout. The interludes are the obvious exceptions, because, well, I couldn't help myself. I hope it doesn't affect your tip calculations.

So with all that said, please indulge me as I must point out a couple of things that were ironic in pursuing this project.

The first is that although there are literally dozens of restaurants covered in these pages, I never ate at many of them. Obviously, I couldn't have patronized the eateries that were in Fairfield before my time (my family moved here in 1976), like Loren's Fountain and Sara's Pancake House. But I just never went to those that were here, like Muffin Treat, the Hut, Sno-Man and others. Most of this was due to me being a kid, and when we ate out, I went where my family took me. My parents had five constantly hungry boys, so the one place we did frequent was Smorga Bob's (and no, we did not steal any chicken).

The other ironic thing is that for the most part, I would now definitely not eat at most of the restaurants featured here, as I am a whole-foods, plant-based eater and have been for the past couple of years. I don't bring this up to be preachy or anything; it's just to say that I am able to compartmentalize my memories and respect and identify with those of others, even though I don't eat that food today. I can cherish lunchtime Armijo memories with friends driving down to A&W and getting a Papa Burger in a basket washed down with an ice-cold mug of root beer and still choose to fuel my body quite differently today.

Now that I've got that off my chest, let me just say that I am aware that an experienced restaurant server allows guests to savor, digest and reflect on their meal. It is my hope that some of the places covered have sparked fires of recognition and remembrance that were warm and wonderful and that you are left with a desire to return.

I also hope that there were some stories about the Fairfield (and Suisun City) restauranteurs that resonated with you on a deeper level than just the sharing of food. Personally, the Mint Grill/the Park Inn owner Yozo Ikenaga's did that for me. When I learned his story, I was upset that this man who was a pillar of the local community was later vilified simply because of his race and nationality in the tumult of the times. I definitely understand that there were incredible stressors during that era, but I still was moved to anger and sadness.

I find it interesting that Jimmie Ciambetti, who ran the Mint with his wife, Bea, was an Italian national. During World War II, Italy was part of the Axis powers the Allied forces were fighting. Unlike Yozo Ikenaga, Ciambetti wasn't arrested by the FBI and sent to a camp. According to his grandson Jimmy Harter, he just had a curfew and had to be off the streets by nightfall.

All of the looking back during the writing of this book made me think of looking forward at the people who will be looking back later. What I mean is, I wonder which Fairfield restaurants people will be reminiscing about in a book like this, say, forty years from now. (They will still have books then, because I have seen both Captain Kirk and Captain Picard reading them).

I think those restaurants would include Evelyn's Big Italian, Hot Stone Korean Kitchen, Chez Soul, Teriyaki House, Rod-Sap Thai Lao Kitchen, El Azteca, C J Fusion, Chicken Express, Yo Sushi, Ohana Hawaiian Barbecue, JJ Fish and Chicken, Favela's Mexican Grill and, in Suisun City, La Cabaña, Babs Delta Diner, the Joy of Eating and the Athenian Grill, among others.

I didn't include iconic Fairfield eateries Joe's Buffet and Dave's Giant Hamburgers because both of those restaurants will still be around forty years from now, of course.

I imagine that sharing about how wonderful the food, service, atmosphere and owners were will permeate those future memories as they have in this book, but I do suspect one thing will be different. There will be many more photographs of the actual food served available in the historical record (last time I use that term) of the future. That's because back in the '50s, '60s, '70s and '80s, folks didn't routinely carry their Brownie, Instamatic or Polaroid cameras into restaurants and take snapshots of their meals before eating.

One thing that will persist as time marches on is the imprinting on folks' memories of eating at specific times in specific places with specific people.

While it can take hours to completely digest a meal eaten in a restaurant so that it becomes fuel for the body, the memories of the people, the place and the event often remain to nourish the soul for a lifetime.

What Is There Now?

Businesses fold and move all the time, but the following is a 2022 snapshot of the establishments located where some bygone restaurants once stood.

A&W Drive-In, 100 East Tabor: Little Caesar's Pizza

The Acacia/The Office/Merlyn's/Johnnie's House of Ribs, 150 Acacia Street: vacant

Airline Café, 844 Texas Street: Straight or Knot Beauty Salon

Baskin-Robbins, 2125 North Texas Street: vacant

Black Swan, Highway 40 two miles west of Fairfield: Hopkins Acura of Fairfield

Chateau Café/Mr. Ed's/David's English Fish and Chips, 419 Texas Street: Solano County parking lot

Colonial Kitchen, 431 Union Avenue: Parking lot for Solano County Probation Department

Colony Kitchen, 2890 Travis Boulevard: Bintoh Thai Boba Cha

Dairy Belle Freeze, 1615 West Texas Street: Jelly Donut

Dan & Ruth's Café, 2982 Rockville Road: El Pitayo Mexican Restaurant

Dari-Delite/Crunchy's, 2260 North Texas Street: Latino Beauty Salon

Dick's/BJ's/Fairfield Express/Tony Roma's, 1620 Pennsylvania Avenue: North American Mental Health Services

Firehouse Deli Café, 620 Jackson Street: vacant

Foster's Old Fashion Freeze, 1430 North Texas Street: Yo Sushi

Happy Steak, 1767 North Texas Street: Rod-Sap Thai Lao Kitchen

Hi-Fi Drive-In, 1513 West Texas Street: Subway

Holiday Inn, 1350 Holiday Lane: Courtyard by Marriott Fairfield Napa Valley Area

The Hut, 2027 North Texas Street: 707 Motors

Johanne's Hot Dogs, 1708 West Texas Street: Karinderya ni Joshua at Arya

Johnson's Pastries and Cafeteria, 811 Texas Street: Guadalajara Fruit Bar

Loren's Fountain, 801 Texas Street: Fairfield Cigar and Vape

Lyon's: 2390 North Texas Street: Benicia Grill 2

Miss Bea's Mint, 609 Main Street, Suisun City: Waterfront Comics

Mr. Steak, 2160 North Texas Street: Les Schwab Tire Center

Muffin Treat, 3333 North Texas Street: Texas Roadhouse

Octo Inn, 2201 Boynton Avenue: Freedom Dental

Sara's Pancake House/Sunrise/Sandy's 101 Omelettes, 1720 North Texas Street: Your Town's Café

Sherwood Forest/Lord Jim's/Fairfield Landing/Hungry Hunter, 2440 Martin Road: vacant

Sid's Drive-In, 1513 North Texas Street: Office building at 1545 that used to be Heart Federal Savings

Smorga Bob's, 1720 West Texas Street: Praise Covenant Church

Sno-White/Sno-Man Drive-In, 530 Union Avenue: Superior Court/Solano County Sheriff's Office

Bibliography

Books

Allen, John S. *The Omnivorous Mind: Our Revolving Relationship with Food.* Cambridge, MA: Harvard University Press, 2012.

Armijo High School. *La Mezcla Yearbooks.* Fairfield, CA: various years.

Fairfield High School. *Talon Yearbooks.* Fairfield, CA, various years.

Moss, Michael. *Hooked: Food, Free Will, and How the Food Giants Exploit Our Addictions.* New York: Random House, 2021.

Polk City Directories. Fairfield, CA: various years.

Sausalito Historical Society. *Images of America: Sausalito.* Charleston, SC: Arcadia Publishing, 2005.

Walker, John R. *The Restaurant: From Concept to Operation.* Hoboken, NJ: Wiley, 2013.

Websites

Ancestry.com
https://www.ancestry.com/

Brainy Quote
https://www.brainyquote.com/

City of Fairfield Resolutions and Ordinances
https://www.fairfield.ca.gov/gov/city_council/resolutions_and_ordinances

"I Grew Up in Fairfield, Too," Facebook group
https://www.facebook.com/groups/fairfieldyears

Newspapers.com
https://www.newspapers.com/

Pixabay
https://pixabay.com/

Microfilm

Daily Republic microfilm, Fairfield Civic Center Library.

Index

About the Author

Tony Wade came to Fairfield in 1976 when he was twelve years old and never left. He attended Grange Intermediate, Armijo High School and Solano Community College. In 2006, Wade began writing columns for the local newspaper the *Daily Republic* as a freelance writer. In 2011, he became an accidental historian when he began writing his "Back in the Day" columns that he describes as "kinda, sorta about local history." He is the older brother of longtime *Fairfield Daily Republic* columnist Kelvin Wade and lives in Fairfield with his wife, Beth, and their Chiweenie, Chunky Tiberius Wade. Tony Wade's first book, *Growing Up in Fairfield California*, was published by The History Press in 2021.

Visit us at
www.historypress.com